NS Simulator for Beginners

Synthesis Lectures on Communication Networks

Editor
Jean Walrand, *University of California, Berkeley*

Synthesis Lectures on Communication Networks is an ongoing series of 50- to 100-page publications on topics on the design, implementation, and management of communication networks. Each lecture is a self-contained presentation of one topic by a leading expert. The topics range from algorithms to hardware implementations and cover a broad spectrum of issues from security to multiple-access protocols. The series addresses technologies from sensor networks to reconfigurable optical networks.
The series is designed to:

- Provide the best available presentations of important aspects of communication networks.

- Help engineers and advanced students keep up with recent developments in a rapidly evolving technology.

- Facilitate the development of courses in this field.

NS Simulator for Beginners
Eitan Altman and Tania Jiménez
2011

Network Games: Theory, Models, and Dynamics
Ishai Menache and Asuman Ozdaglar
2011

An Introduction to Models of Online Peer-to-Peer Social Networking
George Kesidis
2010

Stochastic Network Optimization with Application to Communication and Queueing Systems
Michael J. Neely
2010

Scheduling and Congestion Control for Wireless and Processing Networks
Libin Jiang and Jean Walrand
2010

Performance Modeling of Communication Networks with Markov Chains
Jeonghoon Mo
2010

Communication Networks: A Concise Introduction
Jean Walrand and Shyam Parekh
2010

Path Problems in Networks
John S. Baras and George Theodorakopoulos
2010

Performance Modeling, Loss Networks, and Statistical Multiplexing
Ravi R. Mazumdar
2009

Network Simulation
Richard M. Fujimoto, Kalyan S. Perumalla, and George F. Riley
2006

NS Simulator for Beginners

Eitan Altman and Tania Jiménez

www.morganclaypool.com

ISBN: 9781608456925   paperback
ISBN: 9781608456932   ebook

DOI 10.2200/S00397ED1V01Y201112CNT010

A Publication in the Morgan & Claypool Publishers series
SYNTHESIS LECTURES ON COMMUNICATION NETWORKS

Lecture #10
Series Editor: Jean Walrand, *University of California, Berkeley*
Series ISSN
Synthesis Lectures on Communication Networks
Print 1935-4185   Electronic 1935-4193

NS Simulator for Beginners

Eitan Altman
INRIA, Sophia Antipolis, France

Tania Jiménez
LIA, University of Avignon, France

SYNTHESIS LECTURES ON COMMUNICATION NETWORKS #10

MORGAN & CLAYPOOL PUBLISHERS

ABSTRACT

NS-2 is an open-source discrete event network simulator which is widely used by both the research community as well as by the people involved in the standardization protocols of IETF. The goal of this book is twofold: on one hand to learn how to use the NS-2 simulator, and on the other hand, to become acquainted with and to understand the operation of some of the simulated objects using NS-2 simulations. The book is intended to help students, engineers or researchers who need not have much background in programming or who want to learn through simple examples how to analyse some simulated objects using NS-2. Simulations may differ from each other in many aspects: the applications, topologies, parameters of network objects (links, nodes) and protocols used, etc. The first chapter §1 is a general introduction to the book, where the importance of NS-2 as a tool for a good comprehension of networks and protocols is stated. In the next chapters (§4, §5, §6, §7, §8 and §9) we present special topics as TCP, RED, etc., using NS-2 as a tool for better understanding the protocols. We provide in the appendices a review of Random Variables §A and Confidence Intervals §B, as well as a first sketch for using the new NS-3 simulator §C.

KEYWORDS

NS-2 simulator, TCP simulation, simulation traces, network simulation, tcl

To our children Einat and Daniel.

Contents

Preface

The NS-2 simulator covers a very large number of applications, of protocols, of network types, of network elements and of traffic models. We call these "simulated objects". The goal of this book is twofold: on one hand to learn how to use the NS-2 simulator, and on the other hand, to become acquainted with and to understand the operation of some of the simulated objects using NS-2 simulations. This book provides therefore not only some basics and description of the NS-2 simulator, but also a description of the simulated objects. Finally, we focus on the analysis of the behavior of the simulated objects using NS-2 simulations.

The book is intended to help students, engineers or researchers who need not have much background in programming or who want to learn through simple examples how to analyse some simulated objects using NS-2. For that purpose, we provide a large number of scripts that can be used by the reader so as to start programming immediately. For readers who are interested to learn from examples, we should mention that a very large number of examples are already available in the software package of the NS-2 simulator[1]. Other tutorials containing many examples are available electronically: Marc Greis's tutorial[2] and the tutorial by Jae Chung and Mark Claypool[3].

For a much deeper study of the NS-2 simulator, one should refer to the NS-2 manual which is maintained up-to-date at `http://www.isi.edu/nsnam/ns/`, or to `http://www.nsnam.org/docs/release/manual/singlehtml/index.html` for the NS-3 manual.

We present in this book many simple (but hopefully useful) scenarios for simulations. Simulations may differ from each other in many aspects: the applications, topologies, parameters of network objects (links, nodes) and protocols used, etc. We do not aim at being exhaustive; instead, we present what we consider to be "typical" examples. If one needs a more exhaustive description of NS-2, one may find it very useful to consult the manual. An alternative simple way to know about other possibilities for choosing network elements, network protocols or their parameters, application parameters, etc., is to look directly at the library files that define them[4]. For example, the definitions of mobile nodes could be found in the file *ns-mobilenode.tcl*, those describing queueing disciplines and parameters in the file *ns-queue.tcl*, etc. Default parameters can be found at the file *ns-default.tcl*. Note: to know which default object is related to which command, one may need to check the file *ns-lib.tcl* as we shall see in an example in Section 2.2.

The book is organized in 10 chapters and 3 appendices. The first chapter §1 is a general introduction to the book, where the importance of NS-2 as a tool for a good comprehension of networks

---

[1] It typically appears in the directory ns-2/tcl/ex, where directory "ns-2" could have other longer names that depend on the NS-2 release, e.g. "ns-2.34"

[2] `http://www.isi.edu/nsnam/ns/tutorial/index.html`

[3] `http://nile.wpi.edu/NS/`

[4] `ns-allinone-2.34/ns-2.34/tcl/lib`

and protocols is stated. This chapter also offers a small introduction to the Tcl programming. The chapter §2 give the information that allows one to create a first simple NS-2 script. Chapter §3 is about tracing in NS-2 and how to exploit the traces. In the next chapters (§4, §5, §6, §7, §8 and §9) we present special topics as TCP, RED, etc., using NS-2 as a tool for better understanding the protocols. In the last chapter §10 we briefly explain how to add new classes to the NS-2 architecture. We provide in the appendices a review of Random Variables §A and Confidence Intervals §B, as well as a first sketch for using the new NS-3 simulator §C.

For the last ten years, we have been using the first edition of this book in our courses on simulations. We had written it for our students in ULA (University de Los Andes), Mérida, Venezuela, and have reused this material in courses given in the University of Nice Sophia-Antipolis. Our goal has been not only to learn how to simulate, but also to teach networking by simulating the network protocols. We hope that this book, along with the many programs that are available for free download, will be helpful and useful for students, researchers and engineers.

Eitan Altman and Tania Jiménez
November 2011

CHAPTER 1

Introduction

NS-2 is probably the simulator that has had the largest impact on the development of the Internet. It has served as a tool for exploring the Internet, for discovering properties of proposed protocols, for identifying problems and for testing proposed solutions. It has also been used as a verification tool for proposed analytical models. It has accompanied the Internet and the work of the IETF (Internet Engineering Task Force.)[1]

The NS simulator has been distributed as a free and open source software. This was in line with the spirit of the development of the Internet and its protocols. Indeed, access to the IETF work and standards was much more open than that of the standardization committees of the competing A.T.M. architecture, the ATM forum and the I.T.U. In particular, the contributions to the IETF and its standards have been available on-line and free, unlike the standards of the ATM forum and the ITU.

The open source nature of the NS simulator has allowed thousands of students, engineers and researchers to contribute scripts and patches. This allowed NS-2 to evolve, to be always in the forefront with respect to IETF recommendations, and to serve as a widely available tool for innovation. The strength of NS simulator is partly due to this wide range of volunteer based development of scripts and of patches by many users around the world.

The development of NS-2 has been funded by the DARPA VINT (Virtual InterNetwork Testbed) project from 1997-2000, by DARPA SAMAN (Simulation Augmented by Measurement and Analysis for Networks) and NSF CONSER (Collaborative Simulation for Education and Research) from 2000-2004.

1.1 NS-2 AS A TOOL FOR DESIGNING INTERNET PROTOCOLS

Below are some examples that illustrate the involvement of the NS-2 simulator in the development of protocols and in the work of the IETF.

In 1996, which is the year when NS-2 was released, S. Floyd published a simulation-based comparison of various early versions of TCP [25].

RFC 2415[2] is concerned directly with simulation studies of the initial TCP window size, and all simulations were done using NS-2.

---

[1]The IETF is the main standardization body for Internet protocols.
[2]RFCs are the official documents that the IETF issues. RFC stands for "Request For Comments."

These, as well as much other research relevant to IETF work on TCP over satellite links, are overviewed in RFC 2760 [7].

Ad-hoc networks: NS-2 has often been used in the design or validation of routing protocols for ad-hoc networks. The Optimized Link State Routing Protocol (OLSR) for ad-hoc networks was standardized in RFC 3626. It was proposed by two INRIA researchers, Clausen and Jacquet, who developed in parallel an open source patch for NS-2 that is compatible with this RFC, and which is available on the OLSR page, see `hipercom.inria.fr/olsr`, along with five other implementations of the protocol in NS-2 by other groups.

Comparisons of various routing protocols in ad-hoc networks can be found, e.g., in [53] and [16]. The authors of the latter paper had been involved in the work of the IETF on the standardization of the Dynamic Source Routing (DSR) routing protocol.

TCP friendly schemes: RFC 3448, 4828, and 5348 are RFCs that are concerned with the TCP Friendly Rate Control (TFRC). Both experimentation and simulations in NS-2 were used when developing this TCP friendly protocol.

DiffServ protocols were introduced as RFCs along with validation using NS-2 simulations (e.g., RFC 2598 by V. Jacobson, Nichols and Poduri, 1999).

Comparison of **reliable multicast protocols** using the NS-2 simulator are available in [31]. It appeared in 1998, which is also the year during which the IETF adopted RFC 2357 [42] on that same topic.

An **evaluation test suite** for the initial evaluation of any proposed TCP modifications has been developed and made available [12]. The authors write "The goal of the test suite is to allow researchers quickly and easily to evaluate their proposed TCP extensions in simulators and testbeds using a common set of well-defined, standard test cases, in order to compare and contrast proposals against standard TCP as well as other proposed modifications. This test suite is not intended to result in an exhaustive evaluation of a proposed TCP modification or new congestion control mechanism. Instead, the focus is on quickly and easily generating an initial evaluation report that allows the networking community to understand and discuss the behavioural aspects of a new proposal, in order to guide further experimentation that will be needed to fully investigate the specific aspects of a new proposal." The authors proposed an NS-2 implementation of this suite. They end the paper with the following invitation:"We incite others to contribute implementations on other simulator platforms such as OMNeT++ and OpNet".

In [17], the authors, who study the behavior of the RED (Random Early Discard) gateway using NS-2 simulations, write (already in the abstract) "The ns-2 simulator is the only viable simulation tool accepted by industry for verification purposes."

1.2   NS-2, NS-3 AND OTHER SIMULATORS

The simulator NS-2 has had a smooth transition from the NS-1 version, which had a similar architecture; NS-2 was designed to be backward compatible with scripts written in NS-1. In contrast, the gap between the architectures of NS-2 and NS-3 is very large and NS-3 is not backward compatible. This suggests that NS-2 will remain for many years a useful tool, with an advantage of having huge amount of accessible open source software that had been developed during the last decade and not yet ported to NS-3.

The open source nature of NS-2 and the community-based development practices of NS-2 which were one of the main sources for its rapid development, are expected to continue with the NS-3 version. The reference [34] presents the following: "The main goal of the NS-3 project is to produce a discrete event network simulator for Internet systems, with an emphasis on layers 2-4 of the network stack, targeted primarily for research and educational use. The following goals are also important:

- The project should adopt community-oriented open source development practices.

- The simulator should be distributed as free and open source software, and should leverage and permit inclusion of other free and open source networking software.

- The simulator should be architected for scalability, extensibility, modularity, emulation, and clarity (of design), and should be well documented.

- Core models should be well tested and validated.

- The project should develop a set of canonical simulation based experiments for use in networking courseware."

We next present some references that compare the performance of several simulators. In [36] the author writes: "From the descriptions and the conclusions drawn by the reference papers, it can be concluded that NS-2 and OMNeT++ are the best choices for research. NS-2, is the most popular simulator for academic research, is generally criticized for its complicated architecture. But, its large use by the community makes up for it since there are lots of people helping each other with their problems through the use of mailing lists and forums. OMNeT++ is gaining popularity in academic and industrial world. Unlike NS-2, OMNeT++ has a well-designed simulation engine and supports hierarchical modeling, so it is better for development. Also, OMNeT++'s powerful GUI gives it a certain edge. However, OMNeT++ lacks the abundance of external models and user base NS-2 has. OPNET Modeler is also a good, complete solution; but, it caters to industrial researchers, people who need an extensive set of built-in reliable models for constructing credible simulations in a quick way, rather than academic researchers."

Figure 1.1 provides the conclusions drawn in [41] from its comparison between NS-2, Opnet, and J-Sim, simulators that are perhaps considered the leading ones.

Name/Version	OPNET Modeler 10.0.A	ns-2 2.27	J-Sim (formerly JavaSim) 1.3
Availability	Highly expensive, commercial software (no publicly available trial). Available with source code for simulation modules (except for restricted protocols)	Open-source software, available with full source code, validation tests and examples	Open-source software, available with full source code, and examples
Support	- excellent manual - excellent manual - source code and examples	- good manual - publicly available mailing list - source code and examples	- good manual - publicly available mailing list - source code and examples
Topology/Scenario	- GUI, XML, import (e.g., HP OV) - "scenario" parameters - C/C++	- OTcl scripts (or C++)	- Tcl scripts (or Java) (as of 1.3) - OTcl (or Java) (future releases)
Extensions (components)	- C/C++	- OTcl (higher level) - C++ (lower level)	- Java (as of 1.3) - also OTcl for higher level (future releases)
Simulation mode	- synchronous, single threaded, discrete event queue based, with zero event processing time, fully deterministic - multithreaded, discrete event queue based, with zero event processing time - distributed simulation: HLA (High-Level Arch.)	- synchronous, single threaded, discrete event queue based, with zero event processing time, fully deterministic - parallel/distributed version available (Parallel /Distributed NS, PDNS)	- synchronous, single threaded, with zero event processing time, fully deterministic - multithreaded, "real-time process-based", with event processing time taken into account, non-deterministic
Brief summary (with subjective assessment)	- quite slow, "heavy weight" - expensive commercial software - ready, high-fidelity equipment and protocol models; a "reference" simulator - unique (e.g., military) features; widely used in NATO projects	- fast, quite modern, free - OTcl binding - simplified equipment models - many recent TCP mechanisms implemented for ns-2 - currently most popular in research projects	- scalable, modern, free - Tcl/Jacl binding (OTcl/Jacl) - simplified equipment models - new simulation paradigm (active components)

Figure 1.1: Comparisons between three simulators.

The authors of [40] state: "From the researchers point of view, NS-2 provides very similar results compared to OPNET Modeler, but the freeware version of NS-2 makes it more attractive to a researcher. However, the complete set of OPNET Modeler modules provides more features than Ns-2, and it therefore will be more attractive to network operators." From technical point of view, the reference shows similar performance of both simulators. Surprisingly, a few months later, some of the authors seem to change their mind. They came out with a "clarification" [27] stating that OPNET is better than NS-2.

Reference [30] which is also restricted to NS-2 vs Opnet, states: "The conclusions based on the simulation results for the different MANET scenarios are that the trend of all the metrics in both simulators were rather consistent, although in certain experiments absolute values are quite different. From the results obtained we can conclude that more comparisons between network simulators in general, and between NS-2 and OPNET Modeler in particular, could be done."

Reference [58] compares the performance of OMNET++ with NS-2 and with Opnet in the area of wireless sensor networks. The paper shows that OMNET++ has better performance than both NS-2 and OPNET in terms of simulation time and memory. The paper does not address the reliability of the results obtained by different simulators.

We should finally mention that the quality of the simulation is not only a function of the simulator used but can depend on many other aspects related to the planning, the execution and the analysis of the simulations. Helpful insight can be found in [11]. Figure 1.2 taken from [11] shows, in particular, problems in simulations of Mobile Ad Hoc networks.

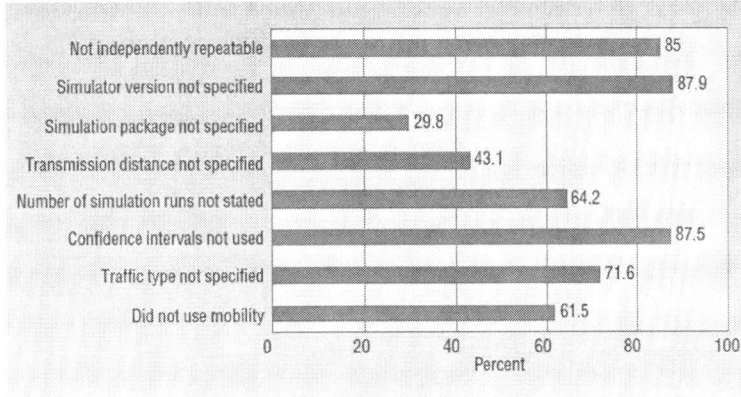

Figure 1.2: Problems in simulations.

1.3   FURTHER BACKGROUND ON NS-2 SIMULATOR

NS-2 simulator is based on two languages: an object oriented simulator, written in C++, and a OTcl (an object oriented extension of Tcl) interpreter, used to execute user command scripts.

NS-2 has a rich library of network and protocol objects. There are two classes of hierarchies: the compiled C++ hierarchy and the interpreted OTcl one, with one to one correspondence between them.

The compiled C++ hierarchy allows us to achieve efficiency in the simulation and faster execution times. This is useful, in particular, for the detailed definition and operation of protocols. This allows one to reduce packet and event processing time.

Then in the OTcl script provided by the user, we can define a particular network topology, the specific protocols and applications that we wish to simulate (whose behavior is already defined in the compiled hierarchy) and the form of the output that we wish to obtain from the simulator. The OTcl can make use of the objects compiled in C++ through an OTcl linkage (using tclCL[3]) that creates a matching of OTcl object for each of the C++. In Chapter 10 we explain how to create new classes on these hierarchies.

NS-2 is a discrete event simulator, where the advance of time depends on the timestamp of events which are maintained by a scheduler. An event is an object in the C++ hierarchy with an unique ID, a scheduled time and the pointer to an object that handles the event. The scheduler keeps an ordered data structure (there are four, but by default NS-2 uses a Calendar scheduler) of the events to be executed and fires them one by one, invoking the handler of the event.

---

[3]TclCL is a Tcl/C++ interface[5].

1.4   TCL AND OTCL PROGRAMMING

Tcl (Tool Command Language) is used by millions of people in the world. It is a language with a very simple syntax and it allows a very easy integration with other languages. Tcl was created by John Ousterhout. The characteristics of this language are the following:

- It allows a fast development

- It provide a graphic interface

- It is compatible with many platforms

- It is flexible for integration

- It is easy to use

- It is free

   Here are some basics of tcl and Otcl programming:

- Assigning a value to a variable is done through the "`set`" command; for example: "`set b 0`" assigns to the variable b the value of 0. This is equivalent to "b=0" in C, for example.

- When we wish to use the value assigned to a variable, we should use a $ sign before the variable. For example, if we want to assign to variable x the value that variable a has, then we should write: "`set x $a`".

- A mathematical operation is done using the expression command. For example, if we wish to assign to a variable x the sum of values of some variables a and b, we should write "`set x [expr $a + $b]`".

- In Tcl the variables are not typed, so a variable can be a string or an integer depending on the value you assign to it. For example, assume that we want to print the result of the division 1/60. If we write
  `puts "[expr 1/60]"`, then the result will be 0. To have the correct result, we need to indicate that we do not work with integers, and should thus type
  `puts "[expr 1.0/60.0]"`

- The sign # starts a commented line that is not part of the program, so the tcl interpreter will not execute this line.

- To create a file, one has to give it a name, say "filename", and to assign a pointer to it that will be used within the tcl program in order to relate to it, say "file1". This is done with the command: `set file1 [open filename w]`.

- The command `puts` is used for printing an output. Note: each time the "`puts`" command is used, a new line is started. To avoid a new line, one has to add `-nonewline` after the "`puts`" command. If we want to print into a file (say the one we defined above), we type `puts $file1` `"text"`. Tabulating is done by inserting `\t`. For example, if a variable, say x, has the value 2 and we type `puts $file1 "x t $x"` then this will print a line into the file whose name is "filename" with two elements: "x" and "2" separated by a tabulator space.

- Execution of a UNIX command: is done by typing "exec" and then the command. For example, we may want NS-2 to initiate the display of a curve whose data are given in a two column file named "data" within the simulation. This can be done using the xgraph command and will be written as:
```
exec xgraph data &
```
(note that the "&" sign is used to have the command executed in the background).

- The structure of an `if` command is as follows:
```
if { expression } {
    <execute some commands>
} else {
    <execute some commands>
}
```
The `if` command can be nested with other "`if`"s and with "`else`"s that can appear in the "`<execute some commands>`" part. Note that when testing equality, we should use "`==`" and not "`=`". The inequality is written with `!=`.

- Loops have the following form:
```
for { set i 0 } { $i < 5 } { incr i } {
    <execute some commands>
}
```
In this example the commands in the loop will be executed five times. After the `for` the "`{ set i 0 }` declares the variable i that will be used as the counter of the loop and initializes it to 0. The second part between { } is the continuation condition of the loop; it says "do the loop while the counter i is less than 5. The last part of the statement is for declaring the changing in the counter variable; in this case we increment i one by one, but we can also decrement it or use any mathematical expression for increment or decrement the counter instead.

- Tcl allows to create procedures. The procedures can return some value when they contain a "return" command. The general form of a procedure which we name "blue" is
```
proc blue { par1 par2 ... } {
        global var1 var2
        <commands>
        return $something
}
```

The procedure receives some parameters that can be objects, files or variables. In our case these are named par1, par2, etc. These parameters will be used within the procedures with these names. The procedure is called by typing blue x y ... where the values of x and y will be used by the procedure for par1 and par2. If par1 and par2 are changed within the procedure, this will not affect the values of x and y. On the other hand, if we wish the procedure to be able to affect directly variables external to it, we have to declare these variables as "global". In the above example these are var1 and var2.

In the following, we will show how to use these commands through some simple examples of tcl.

Example 1.1   In Listing 1.1 we show an example that presents many arithmetic operations in tcl. The pow expression give the power of variable d to j.

Listing 1.1: Tcl script for arithmetic operations.

```
#Create a procedure
proc test {} {
    set a 12
    set b 15
    set c [expr $a + $b]
    set d [expr [expr $a - $b] * $c]
    puts "c =  $c d =   $d"
    for {set j 0} {$j < 10} {incr j} {
        if {$j < 5} {
            puts "j < 5, pow = [expr pow($d, $j)]"
        } else {
            puts "j >= 5, mod = [expr $d % $j]"
        }
    }
}
#calling the procedure
test
```

Example 1.2   Listing 1.2 is an example of a tcl program for computing all the prime numbers up to a given limit j. For example, to obtain all the prime numbers up to 11 type simply "ns prime.tcl 11". The prime numbers example shows how to use an if command, loops, and a procedure.

The variable argc contains the number of parameters passed to the program. The variable argv is a vector that has the parameters passed to the program (so, argc is the length of argv), and the command lindex allows us to take the case of the vector pointed by the second parameter. So, the line set j [lindex $argv 0] assigns to the variable j the value of the first parameter passed to the program which has been saved on the variable argv.

Listing 1.2: Tcl script for computing prime numbers.

```
#Usage: ns prime.tcl NUMBER
#   NUMBER is the number up to which we want to obtain the prime numbers
#
if {$argc  != 1} {
  #  Must get a single argument or program fails.
  puts stderr "ERROR! ns called with wrong number of arguments!($argc)"
  exit 1
} else {
  set j [lindex $argv 0]
}

proc prime {j} {
          # Computes all the prime numbers till j
          for {set a 2} {$a <= $j} {incr a} {
             set b 0
             for {set i 2} {$i < $a} {incr i} {
                set d [expr fmod($a,$i)]
                if {$d==0} {
                   set b 1}
             }
             if {$b==1} {
                puts "$a is not a prime number"
             } else {
                puts "$a is a prime number"
             }
          }
        }
prime $j
```

Example 1.3   In Listing 1.3 we use a procedure in order to compute the factorial of a number given as a parameter to the main program.

Listing 1.3: Tcl script for computing the factorial of a number.

```
# Usage: ns fact.tcl NUMBER
#          we want to find the factorial of the number NUMBER
#
if {$argc  != 1} {
  #  Must get a single argument or program fails.
  puts stderr "ERROR! ns called with wrong number of arguments!($argc)"
  exit 1
} else {
  set f [lindex $argv 0]
}

proc Factorial {x} {
   for {set result 1} {$x > 1} {set x [expr $x - 1] } {
       set result [expr $result * $x]
   }
return $result
```

```
}
set res [Factorial $f]
puts "Factorial of $f is $res"
```

We explain briefly through an example the Object Programming paradigm in OTcl as illustrated in Listings 1.4 and 1.5. If you don't know an Object Oriented language (like C++ or Java), we recommend to look for documentation beforehand in order to learn how to program using object oriented languages.

Example 1.4   The reserved word `Class` followed by the name of the class is used to declare a new class in OTcl. The methods of the classes are declared using the word `instproc` preceded by the name of the class and followed by the name of the method and its parameters. The method `init` is the constructor of the class. The variable `self` is a pointer to the object itself, like `this` in C++ or Java. To declare the instance variable, OTcl uses the word `instvar`. The word `-superclass` is used for declaring that a class inherits from another one, in the example the Integer class inherits from the Real class.

Listing 1.4: Simple Otcl program using real and integer objects (a).

```
Class Real

Real instproc init {a} {
       $self instvar value_
       set value_ $a
}

Real instproc sum {x} {
       $self instvar value_
       set op "$value_ + [$x set value_] = \t"
       set value_ [expr $value_ +  [$x set value_]]
       puts "$op $value_"
}

Real instproc multiply {x} {
       $self instvar value_
       set op "$value_ * [$x set value_] = \t"
       set value_ [expr $value_ *  [$x set value_]]
       puts "$op $value_"
}

Real instproc divide {x} {
       $self instvar value_
       set op "$value_ / [$x set value_] = \t"
       set value_ [expr $value_ /  [$x set value_]]
       puts "$op $value_"
}

Class Integer -superclass Real

Integer instproc divide {x} {
```

```
$self instvar value_
set op "$value_ / [$x set value_] = \t"
set d [expr $value_ / [$x set value_]]
set value_ [expr round($d)]
puts "$op $value_"
}
```

Listing 1.5: Simple Otcl program using real and integer objects (b).

```
set realA [new Real 12.3]
set realB [new Real 0.5]

$realA sum $realB
$realA multiply $realB
$realA divide $realB

set integerA [new Integer 12]
set integerB [new Integer 5]
set integerC [new Integer 7]

$integerA multiply $integerB
$integerB divide $integerC
```

CHAPTER 2

NS-2 Simulator Preliminaries

In this Chapter we present the first steps that consist of

- Initialization and termination aspects of NS-2 simulator,

- Definition of network nodes, links, queues and topology,

- Definition of agents and applications,

- The nam visualisation tool,

- Tracing, and

- Random Variables.

Some simple examples will be given that will enable us to make the first steps with the NS-2 simulator.

2.1   INITIALIZATION AND TERMINATION

A Tcl script in NS-2 simulation starts with the command:

```
set ns [new Simulator]
```

This line declares a new variable ns using the set Tcl command. You can call this variable whatever you wish, but, in general, people declare it as ns because it is an instance of the Simulator class, so an object. The code [new Simulator] is indeed the instantiation of the class Simulator using the reserved word new. So, using this new variable ns we can use all the methods of the class Simulator that we will see below.

In order to have output files with data on the simulation (trace files) or files used for visualisation (nam files), we need to create the files using the "open" command:

```
#Open the Trace file
set tracefile1 [open out.tr w]
$ns trace-all $tracefile1

#Open the NAM trace file
set namfile [open out.nam w]
$ns namtrace-all $namfile
```

The code above creates a data trace file called "out.tr" and a nam visualisation trace file (for the NAM tool) called "out.nam". Within the tcl script, these files are not called explicitly by their names (out.tr and out.nam), but instead by pointers that are declared above and called "tracefile1" and "namfile," respectively.

The first and fourth lines in the example are only comments; they are not simulation commands. Note that these lines begin with a # symbol. The second line opens the file "out.tr" to be used for writing, declared with the letter "w". The third line uses a simulator method called `trace-all` that has as parameter the name of the file where the traces will be written. With this simulator command we will trace all the events in a specific format that we will explain later in this chapter.

The last line tells the simulator to record all simulation traces in NAM input format.

Note: the commands trace-all and namtrace-all may result in the creation of huge files. If we wish to save space, other trace commands should be used so as to trace only a subset of the simulated events which may be needed. Such commands are described in Section 2.6.

The termination of the program is made using a "`finish`" procedure.

```
#Define a 'finish' procedure
proc finish {} {
        global ns tracefile1 namfile
        $ns flush-trace
        close $tracefile1
        close $namfile
        exec nam out.nam &
        exit 0
}
```

The word `proc` declares a procedure in this case called `finish` and without arguments. The word `global` is used to specify that we are using variables declared outside the procedure. The simulator method "`flush-trace`" will dump the traces on the respective files. The tcl command "`close`" closes the trace files defined before and `exec` executes the nam program for visualisation. Note that we pass the real name of the file of traces to nam and not to the pointer `namfile` because it is an external command. The command `exit` will end the application and return the number 0 as status to the system. Zero is the default for a clean exit. Other values can be used to say that it is an exit because something fails.

At the end of the NS-2 program we should call the procedure "`finish`" and specify at what time the termination should occur. For example,
`$ns at 125.0 "finish"`
will be used to call "`finish`" at time 125 sec. Indeed, the `at` method of the simulator allows us to schedule events explicitly.

The simulation can then begin using the command
`$ns run`

2.2   DEFINITION OF A NETWORK OF LINKS AND NODES

The way to define a node is

```
set n0 [$ns node]
```

We have created a node that is pointed by the variable n0. When we refer to that node in the script, we shall thus write $n0.

Once we define several nodes, we can define the links that connect them. An example of a definition of a link is:

```
$ns duplex-link $n0 $n2 10Mb 10ms DropTail
```

which means that nodes $n0 and $n2 are connected using a bi-directional link that has 10ms of propagation delay and capacity of 10 Mb/sec for each direction.

To define a directional link instead of a bi-directional one, we replace "duplex-link" by "simplex-link".

In NS-2, an output queue of a node is implemented as a part of each link whose input is that node. The definition of the link then includes the way to handle overflow at that queue. In our case, if the buffer capacity of the output queue is exceeded then the last packet to arrive is dropped (DropTail option). Many alternative options exist, such as the RED (Random Early Discard) mechanism, the FQ (Fair Queueing), the DRR (Deficit Round Robin), the Stochastic Fair Queueing (SFQ) and the CBQ (which includes a priority and a round-robin scheduler); we shall return later to the RED mechanism in more detail.

Of course, we should also define the buffer capacity of the queue related to each link. An example would be:

```
#Set Queue Size of link (n0-n2) to 20
$ns queue-limit $n0 $n2 20
```

A simplex link has the form presented in Figure 2.1. A queue overflow is implemented by sending dropped packets to a Null Agent. The TTL object computes the Time To Live parameter[1] for each received packet. A duplex link is constructed from two parallel simplex links.

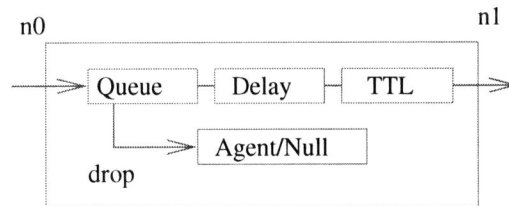

Figure 2.1: A simplex link.

Example 2.1   As an example of a simple network, consider the one depicted in Figure 2.2; this network is defined through the script given in Listing 2.1.

---

[1]Packets have some associated tags which are updated in the network and that indicate how long they can still stay in the network before reaching the destination. When this time expires, then the packet is dropped.

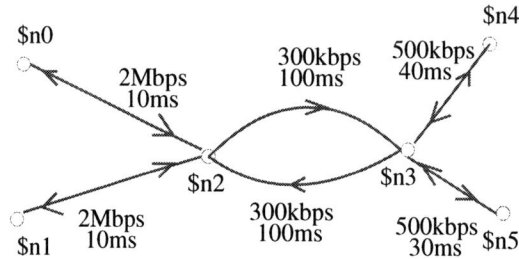

Figure 2.2: Example of a simple network.

Listing 2.1: "Definition nodes links and assigning queue size".

```
#Create six nodes
set n0 [$ns node]
set n1 [$ns node]
set n2 [$ns node]
set n3 [$ns node]
set n4 [$ns node]
set n5 [$ns node]

#Create links between the nodes
$ns duplex-link $n0 $n2 2Mb 10ms DropTail
$ns duplex-link $n1 $n2 2Mb 10ms DropTail
$ns simplex-link $n2 $n3 0.3Mb 100ms DropTail
$ns simplex-link $n3 $n2 0.3Mb 100ms DropTail
$ns duplex-link $n3 $n4 0.5Mb 40ms DropTail
$ns duplex-link $n3 $n5 0.5Mb 30ms DropTail

#Set Queue Size of link (n2-n3) to 20
$ns queue-limit $n2 $n3 20
```

Note that we defined the buffer capacity corresponding to one link only (between n2 and n3). The queues corresponding to all other links have the default value of 50. This default value can be found at ns-default.tcl[2] in the command

```
Queue set limit_ 50
```

How could we find this default? By first checking the file ns-lib.tcl where we find the queue-limit procedure

```
Simulator instproc queue-limit { n1 n2 limit } {
        $self instvar link_
        [$link_([$n1 id]:[$n2 id]) queue] set limit_ $limit
}
```

[2]In ns-allinone-2.XXX/ns-2.XXX/tcl/lib, where XXX stands for the version number, e.g., 34.

in which we see that the queue limit is indeed a method of the simulator that needs three parameters: the two nodes that define the link and the queue limit. There we see that the limit number is given by the variable limit_.

2.3   AGENTS AND APPLICATIONS

Having defined the topology (nodes and links), we should now make traffic flow through them. To that end, we need to define routing (in particular, sources and destinations), the agents (protocols) and applications that use them.

In the previous example, we may wish to run an FTP (File Transfer Protocol)[49] application between node $n0 and $n4, and a CBR (Constant Bit Rate) application between node $n1 and $n5. The Internet protocol used by FTP is TCP/IP (TCP for Transport Control Protocol/Internet Protocol) and the one used by CBR is UDP (User Datagram Protocol). We should first define in Listing 2.2 a TCP agent between the source node $n0 and the destination node $n4 and then the FTP application that uses it. We then define in Listing 2.3 the UDP agent between the source node $n1 and the destination node $n5 and the CBR application that uses it.

2.3.1   FTP OVER TCP

TCP is a dynamic reliable congestion control protocol which will be explained in detail in Chapter 4. It uses acknowledgements created by the destination to know whether packets are well received, lost packets are interpreted as congestion signals; TCP thus requires bidirectional links for the acknowledgements in order to return information to the source.

There are many variants of the TCP protocol, such as Tahoe, Reno, Newreno, Vegas. The type of agent appears in the first line:

```
set tcp [new Agent/TCP]
```

This commands also gives a pointer called "tcp" here to the TCP agent, which is an object in NS-2.

The command $ns attach-agent $n0 $tcp defines the source node of the TCP connection. The command set sink [new Agent/TCPSink] defines the behavior of the destination node of TCP and assigns to it a pointer called sink. We note that in TCP the destination node has an active role in the protocol of generating acknowledgements in order to guarantee that all packets arrive at the destination.

The command $ns attach-agent $n4 $sink defines the destination node. The command $ns connect $tcp $sink finally makes the TCP connection between the source and destination nodes.

TCP has many parameters with initial fixed default values that can be changed if mentioned explicitly. For example, the default TCP packet size has a size of 1000 bytes. This can be changed to another value, say 552 bytes, using the command $tcp set packetSize_ 552.

When we have several flows, we may wish to distinguish them so that we can identify them with different colors in the visualisation part. This is done by the command $tcp set fid_ 1 that assigns to the TCP connection a flow identification of "1"; we shall later give the flow identification of "2" to the UDP connection.

Once the TCP connection is defined, the FTP application is defined over it. This is done in the last three lines in Listing 2.2.

Note that both the TCP agent as well as the FTP application are given pointers: we called the one for the TCP agent "tcp" (but could have used any other name) and the one for FTP we called "ftp".

Listing 2.2: The definition of an FTP application using a TCP agent.

```
#Setup a TCP connection
set tcp [new Agent/TCP]
$ns attach-agent $n0 $tcp
set sink [new Agent/TCPSink]
$ns attach-agent $n4 $sink
$ns connect $tcp $sink
$tcp set fid_ 1
$tcp set packetSize_ 552

#Setup a FTP over TCP connection
set ftp [new Application/FTP]
$ftp attach-agent $tcp
```

2.3.2   CBR OVER UDP

Next we define the UDP connection and the CBR application over it, see Listing 2.3. A UDP source (Agent/UDP) and destination (Agent/Null) is defined in a similar way as in the case of TCP. For the CBR application that uses UDP, the Listing 2.3 shows also how to define the transmission rate and packet size.

Listing 2.3: The definition of a CBR application using a UDP agent.

```
#Setup a UDP connection
set udp [new Agent/UDP]
$ns attach-agent $n1 $udp
set null [new Agent/Null]
$ns attach-agent $n5 $null
$ns connect $udp $null
$udp set fid_ 2

#Setup a CBR over UDP connection
set cbr [new Application/Traffic/CBR]
$cbr attach-agent $udp
$cbr set packetSize_ 1000
$cbr set rate_ 0.01Mb
$cbr set random_ false
```

Instead of defining the rate, in the command $cbr set rate_ 0.01Mb, one can define the time interval between transmission of packets using the command

```
$cbr set interval_ 0.005
```

Other characteristics of CBR are `random_` which is a flag indicating whether or not to introduce random "noise" in the scheduled transmission times. It is "off" by default, and can be set to be "on" by typing

```
$cbr set random_ 1
```

The packet size can be set to some value (in bytes) using

```
$cbr set packetSize_ <packet size>
```

2.3.3   UDP WITH OTHER TRAFFIC SOURCES

We may simulate other types of traffic applications that use the UDP protocol: the exponential on-off traffic source, the Pareto on-off source, and a trace driven source. The Exponential and Pareto sources are declared, respectively, using

```
set source [new Application/Traffic/Exponential]
set source [new Application/Traffic/Pareto]
```

These sources take as parameters `packetSize_` (in bytes), `burst_time_` which defines the average "on" time, `idle_time_` which defines the average "off" time, and `rate_` which determines the transmission rate during the "on" periods. In the Pareto On/Off source we also define the "shape" parameter `shape_`. An example of a Pareto On/Off is given by:

```
set source [new Application/Traffic/Pareto]
$source set packetSize_ 500
$source set burst_time_ 200ms
$source set idle_time_ 400ms
$source set rate_ 100k
$source set shape_ 1.5
```

(For a discussion on random variables, see Section 2.7.)

The trace driven application is defined as follows. We first declare the trace file:

```
set tracefile [new Tracefile]
$tracefile filename <file>
```

Then, we define the application to be trace driven and attach it to that file:

```
set src [new Application/Traffic/Trace]
$src attach-tracefile $tracefile
```

The file should be in binary format and contain inter-packet time in msec and packet size in bytes.

2.4   SCHEDULING EVENTS IN NS-2

NS-2 is a discrete event based simulation. The Tcl script defines when events should occur. The initializing command `set ns [new Simulator]` creates an event scheduler, and events are then scheduled using the format:

```
$ns at <time> <event>
```

The scheduler is started when running NS-2, i.e., through the command $ns run.

In our simple example, we should schedule the beginning and end of the FTP and the CBR applications. This can be done through the following commands:

```
$ns at 0.1 "$cbr start"
$ns at 1.0 "$ftp start"
$ns at 124.0 "$ftp stop"
$ns at 124.5 "$cbr stop"
```

Thus the FTP will be active from time 1.0 till 124.0 and the CBR will be active from time 0.1 till 124.5 (all units are in seconds).

We are now ready to run the whole simulation.

Example 2.2

If our commands were written in a file called "ex1.tcl" (see Listing 2.4), we would have to type "ns ex1.tcl".

Note: in Listing 2.4 we have added at the end another procedure that writes an output file with the instantaneous sizes of the congestion window of TCP at time intervals of 0.1 sec. In the example, the name of the output file is "WinFile". The procedure is a recursive one, after each 0.1 sec it calls itself again. It passes as parameter the TCP source and the file to which we wish to write the output.

Listing 2.4: Script file ex1.tcl.

```
set ns [new Simulator]

$ns color 1 Blue          #Define different colors for data flows (for NAM)
$ns color 2 Red

set tracefile1 [open out.tr w]  #Open the Trace files
set winfile [open WinFile w]
$ns trace-all $tracefile1
set namfile [open out.nam w]
$ns namtrace-all $namfile

proc finish {} {                  #Define a 'finish' procedure
        global ns tracefile1 namfile
        $ns flush-trace
        close $tracefile1
        close $namfile
        exec nam out.nam &
        exit 0
}

set n0 [$ns node]        #Create six nodes
set n1 [$ns node]
set n2 [$ns node]
```

```
set n3 [$ns node]
set n4 [$ns node]
set n5 [$ns node]

$ns duplex-link $n0 $n2 2Mb 10ms DropTail    #Create links between the nodes
$ns duplex-link $n1 $n2 2Mb 10ms DropTail
$ns simplex-link $n2 $n3 0.3Mb 100ms DropTail
$ns simplex-link $n3 $n2 0.3Mb 100ms DropTail
$ns duplex-link $n3 $n4 0.5Mb 40ms DropTail
$ns duplex-link $n3 $n5 0.5Mb 30ms DropTail

$ns duplex-link-op $n0 $n2 orient right-down   #Give node position (for NAM)
$ns duplex-link-op $n1 $n2 orient right-up
$ns simplex-link-op $n2 $n3 orient right
$ns simplex-link-op $n3 $n2 orient left
$ns duplex-link-op $n3 $n4 orient right-up
$ns duplex-link-op $n3 $n5 orient right-down

$ns queue-limit $n2 $n3 20      #Set Queue Size of link (n2-n3) to 20

set tcp [new Agent/TCP]        #Setup a TCP connection
$ns attach-agent $n0 $tcp
set sink [new Agent/TCPSink]
$ns attach-agent $n4 $sink
$ns connect $tcp $sink
$tcp set fid_ 1
$tcp set packetSize_ 552

set ftp [new Application/FTP]   #Setup a FTP over TCP connection
$ftp attach-agent $tcp

#Setup a UDP connection
set udp [new Agent/UDP]
$ns attach-agent $n1 $udp
set null [new Agent/Null]
$ns attach-agent $n5 $null
$ns connect $udp $null
$udp set fid_ 2

set cbr [new Application/Traffic/CBR]   #Setup a CBR over UDP connection
$cbr attach-agent $udp
$cbr set packetSize_ 1000
$cbr set rate_ 0.01Mb
$cbr set random_ false
$ns at 0.1 "$cbr start"
$ns at 1.0 "$ftp start"
$ns at 124.0 "$ftp stop"
$ns at 124.5 "$cbr stop"

# Procedure for plotting window size.  Gets as arguments the name of the tcp
#source node (called "tcpSource") and of output file.
proc plotWindow {tcpSource file} {
        global ns
        set time 0.1
        set now [$ns now]
        set cwnd [$tcpSource set cwnd_]
```

```
        puts $file "$now $cwnd"
        $ns at [expr $now+$time] "plotWindow $tcpSource $file"
}
$ns at 0.1 "plotWindow $tcp $winfile"
$ns at 125.0 "finish"
$ns run
```

2.5   VISUALISATION USING NAM

When we run the example ex1.tcl, the visualisation tool nam will display a 6 nodes network. The location of the nodes could have been chosen at random. In order to reproduce the initial location of the nodes as in Figure 2.2, we added to the tcl script the following lines:

```
#Give node position (for NAM)
$ns duplex-link-op $n0 $n2 orient right-down
$ns duplex-link-op $n1 $n2 orient right-up
$ns simplex-link-op $n2 $n3 orient right
$ns simplex-link-op $n3 $n2 orient left
$ns duplex-link-op $n3 $n4 orient right-up
$ns duplex-link-op $n3 $n5 orient right-down
```

Note: if a random location of nodes is chosen and it is not satisfactory, one can press on the "re-layout" button and then another random location is chosen. One can also edit the location by clicking at the Edit/View button, and then "dragging" each node to its required location (with the help of the mouse).

We note that the nam display shows us with animation the CBR packets (that flow from node 1 to 5) in red, and TCP packets (flowing from node 0 to 4) in blue. TCP ACKs (acknowledgements) that go in the reverse directions are also in blue but are much shorter, since an ACK has a size of 40 bytes whereas the TCP packet is of size 552 bytes. To obtain the colors, we had to define them in the beginning of our script ex1.tcl

```
$ns color 1 Blue
$ns color 2 Red
```

Note that if we already have a nam file, we do not have to run ns in order to view it, but instead type directly the command nam <file name>.

"Snapshots" from the nam visualisations can be printed (into a printer or into a file) by going into the "File" option in the top menu.

Other things that can be done in NAM:

- Coloring nodes: for example if n0 is to appear in red, we write $n0 color red.

- Shape of nodes: by default they are round, but can appear differently. For example one can type $n1 shape box (or instead of "box" one can use "hexagon" or "circle").

- Coloring links: type for example

```
$ns duplex-link-op $n0 $n2 color "green"
```

- Adding and removing marks: We can mark a node at a given time (for example at the same time as we activated some traffic source at that time). For example, we can type:
```
$ns at 2.0 "$n3 add-mark m3 blue box"
$ns at 30.0 "$n3 delete-mark m3"
```

This results in a blue mark that surrounds the node 3 during the time interval [2,30].

- Adding labels: a label can appear on the screen from a given time onwards, e.g., for giving the label "active node" to a node n3 from time 1.2, type:
```
$ns at 1.2 "$n3 label \"active node\""
```

and to give a the label "TCP input link" to link n0-n2 type
```
$ns duplex-link-op $n0 $n2 label "TCP input link"
```

- Adding text: at the bottom frame of the NAM window one can make text appear at a given time. This can be used to describe some event that is scheduled at that time. An example is
```
$ns at 5 "$ns trace-annotate \"packet drop\""
```

- One may further add in NAM a monitoring of the queue size. For example, to monitor the input queue of the link n2-n3, one types $ns simplex-link-op $n2 $n3 queuePos 0.5

(All the examples refer to objects defined in ex1.tcl.)

The graphic interface of NAM is shown in figure 2.3.

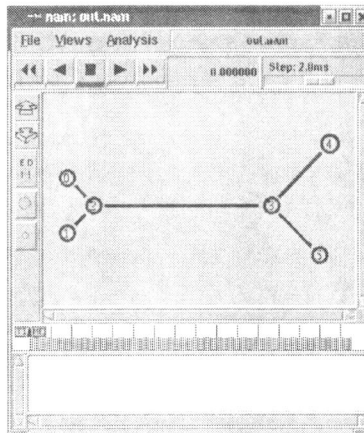

Figure 2.3: NAM graphic interface.

NOTE: It is worth to note that the example ex1.tcl is a "toy" example. With this configuration, we cannot have losses, because the default receiver window (window_) in NS-2 is 20 packets, and because of the bandwidth delay product for this example.

2.6   TRACING

2.6.1   TRACING OBJECTS

NS-2 simulation can produce both the visualisation trace (for NAM) as well as an ascii file trace corresponding to the events registered at the network.

When we use tracing (as mentioned in Section 2.1), ns inserts four objects in the link: EnqT, DeqT, RecvT and DrpT, as indicated in Figure 2.4.

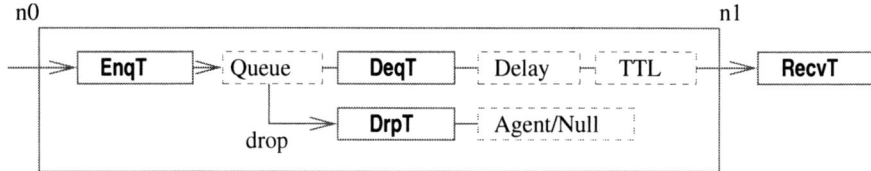

Figure 2.4: Tracing objects in a simplex link.

EnqT registers information concerning a packet that arrives and is queued at the input queue of the link. If the packet overflows, then information concerning the dropped packet are handled by DrpT. DeqT registers information at the instant the packet is dequed. Finally, RecvT gives us information about packets that have been received at the output of the link.

NS-2 allows us to get more information than through the above tracing. One way is by using queue monitoring. This is described at the end of Section 4.3.

2.6.2   STRUCTURE OF TRACE FILES

When tracing into an output ascii file, the trace is organized into 12 fields as follows in Figure 2.5.

Figure 2.5: Fields appearing in a trace.

The meanings of the fields are:

1. The first field is the event type. It is given by one of four possible symbols $r, +, -, d$, which correspond respectively to receive (at the output of the link), enqueued, dequeued and dropped.

2. The second field gives the time at which the event occurs.

3. The third field gives the input node of the link at which the event occurs.

4. The fourth field gives the output node of the link at which the event occurs.

5. The fifth field gives the packet type (for example, CBR, or TCP). The type corresponds to the name that we gave to those applications. For example, the TCP application in Listing 2.2 is called "tcp".

6. The sixth field gives the packet size.

7. Some flags follow (that we shall see later).

8. This is the flow id (fid) of IPv6 that a user can set for each flow at the input OTcl script. One can further use this field for analysis purposes; it is also used when specifying stream color for the NAM display.

9. This is the source address given in the form of "node.port".

10. This is the destination address, given in the same form.

11. This is the network layer protocol's packet sequence number. Even though UDP implementations in a real network do not use sequence number, NS-2 keeps track of UDP packet sequence number for analysis purposes.

12. The last field shows the unique id of the packet.

As an example, consider the first lines of the trace produced by running the script ex1.tcl given in Listing 2.4.

Listing 2.5: First lines of the trace file "out.tr" produced by ex1.tcl.

```
+ 0.1 1 2 cbr 1000 ------- 2 1.0 5.0 0 0
- 0.1 1 2 cbr 1000 ------- 2 1.0 5.0 0 0
r 0.114 1 2 cbr 1000 ------- 2 1.0 5.0 0 0
+ 0.114 2 3 cbr 1000 ------- 2 1.0 5.0 0 0
- 0.114 2 3 cbr 1000 ------- 2 1.0 5.0 0 0
r 0.240667 2 3 cbr 1000 ------- 2 1.0 5.0 0 0
+ 0.240667 3 5 cbr 1000 ------- 2 1.0 5.0 0 0
- 0.240667 3 5 cbr 1000 ------- 2 1.0 5.0 0 0
r 0.286667 3 5 cbr 1000 ------- 2 1.0 5.0 0 0
+ 0.9 1 2 cbr 1000 ------- 2 1.0 5.0 1 1
- 0.9 1 2 cbr 1000 ------- 2 1.0 5.0 1 1
r 0.914 1 2 cbr 1000 ------- 2 1.0 5.0 1 1
+ 0.914 2 3 cbr 1000 ------- 2 1.0 5.0 1 1
- 0.914 2 3 cbr 1000 ------- 2 1.0 5.0 1 1
+ 1 0 2 tcp 40 ------- 1 0.0 4.0 0 2
- 1 0 2 tcp 40 ------- 1 0.0 4.0 0 2
r 1.01016 0 2 tcp 40 ------- 1 0.0 4.0 0 2
+ 1.01016 2 3 tcp 40 ------- 1 0.0 4.0 0 2
- 1.01016 2 3 tcp 40 ------- 1 0.0 4.0 0 2
r 1.040667 2 3 cbr 1000 ------- 2 1.0 5.0 1 1
+ 1.040667 3 5 cbr 1000 ------- 2 1.0 5.0 1 1
- 1.040667 3 5 cbr 1000 ------- 2 1.0 5.0 1 1
r 1.086667 3 5 cbr 1000 ------- 2 1.0 5.0 1 1
r 1.111227 2 3 tcp 40 ------- 1 0.0 4.0 0 2
```

```
+ 1.111227 3 4 tcp 40 ------- 1 0.0 4.0 0 2
- 1.111227 3 4 tcp 40 ------- 1 0.0 4.0 0 2
r 1.151867 3 4 tcp 40 ------- 1 0.0 4.0 0 2
+ 1.251867 4 3 ack 40 ------- 1 4.0 0.0 0 3
- 1.251867 4 3 ack 40 ------- 1 4.0 0.0 0 3
+ 1.251867 4 3 ack 40 ------- 1 4.0 0.0 0 3
- 1.251867 4 3 ack 40 ------- 1 4.0 0.0 0 3
r 1.292507 4 3 ack 40 ------- 1 4.0 0.0 0 3
+ 1.292507 3 2 ack 40 ------- 1 4.0 0.0 0 3
- 1.292507 3 2 ack 40 ------- 1 4.0 0.0 0 3
r 1.393573 3 2 ack 40 ------- 1 4.0 0.0 0 3
+ 1.393573 2 0 ack 40 ------- 1 4.0 0.0 0 3
- 1.393573 2 0 ack 40 ------- 1 4.0 0.0 0 3
r 1.403733 2 0 ack 40 ------- 1 4.0 0.0 0 3
+ 1.403733 0 2 tcp 552 ------- 1 0.0 4.0 1 4
- 1.403733 0 2 tcp 552 ------- 1 0.0 4.0 1 4
+ 1.403733 0 2 tcp 552 ------- 1 0.0 4.0 2 5
- 1.405941 0 2 tcp 552 ------- 1 0.0 4.0 2 5
r 1.415941 0 2 tcp 552 ------- 1 0.0 4.0 1 4
```

2.6.3   TRACING A SUBSET OF EVENTS

In Section 2.1 we already mentioned how to trace all simulated events. We now indicate ways to trace only a subset of these events.

The first way is by replacing the command $ns trace-all <filename> by the command $ns trace-queue. For example, we can type

```
$ns trace-queue $n2 $n3 $file1
```

which will result in an output trace file that contains only events that occurred over the link between nodes n2 and n3 (these are nodes defined in Table 2.1). (A similar command can be used for the nam trace, using namtrace-queue instead of trace-queue.) The trace-queue line should appear of course after the definition of the links, i.e., after the script part of Table 2.1.

It is also possible to filter events using UNIX commands within the tcl script. This will be discussed in Section 3.6.

2.7   RANDOM VARIABLES

Random Variables (RVs) with different distributions can be created in NS-2. Due to its important role in traffic modeling and in network simulation, we briefly recall the definitions and moments of main random variables in Appendix A. For more background, one can consult, e.g., http://www.xycoon.com/.

2.7.1   SEEDS AND GENERATORS

In addition to its distribution, there are other aspects that we need to be concerned with when simulating a random variable:

- Do we want to obtain the same value of the random variable when running the simulation again (possibly varying some other parameters of simulations)? This would allow us to compare directly, for a single random set of events, how the simulated results depend on some physical parameters (such as link delays or queue length).

- Often we need random variables to be independent of each other.

The generation of random variables uses a seed (which is some number that we write in the tcl script). The seed value of 0 results in the generation of a new random variable each time we run the simulation, so if we wish to have the same generated random variables for different simulations, we would have to save the generated random variables. In contrast, if we use other seeds then each time we run the simulation, the same sequence of random variables that are generated in a simulation will be generated.

In ns-2, if we use different generators with the same seed and the same distribution, they will create the same values of random variables (unless the seed is zero). We shall see this in an example below.

2.7.2   CREATING RANDOM VARIABLES IN NS-2

We first create three new random generators and go to the substream corresponding to the replication number $rep which is a variable declared before.

```
set rng1 [new RNG]
set rng2 [new RNG]
set rng3 [new RNG]

for {set i 1} {$i < $rep} {incr i} {
    $rng1 next-substream;
    $rng2 next-substream;
    $rng3 next-substream;
}
```

Then when actually creating a random variable, we have to define its distribution type and its parameters. We give several examples below: we create RVs with Pareto, Constant, Uniform, Exponential and HyperExponential distributions.

1. **Pareto Distribution.** A Pareto distributed RV, say $r1$, is constructed by specifying its expectation and its shape parameter β, the default values are 1.0 and 1.5, respectively.

   ```
   set r1 [new RandomVariable/Pareto]
   $r1 use-rng $rng1
   $r1 set avg_ 10.0
   $r1 set shape_ 1.2
   ```

2. **Constant.** A degenerated random variable is the constant which equals to its value:

```
set r2 [new RandomVariable/Constant]
$r2 use-rng $rng2
$r2 set val_ 5.0
```

3. **Uniform distribution.** It is defined through the smallest and largest point in its support:

```
set r3 [new RandomVariable/Uniform]
$r3 use-rng $rng3
$r3 set min_ 0.0
$r3 set max_ 10.0
```

4. **Exponential distribution.** It is defined through its average value:

```
set r4 [new RandomVariable/Exponential]
$r4 use-rng $rng1
$r4 set avg_ 5
```

5. **Hyperexponential distribution.** It is defined as follows:

```
set r5 [new RandomVariable/HyperExponential]
$r5 use-rng $rng2
$r5 set avg_ 1.0
$r5 set cov_ 4.0
```

Example 2.3   Next we present a small program (rv1.tcl) that tests Pareto distributed random variables with different seeds and generators but with the same Pareto distribution. It is given in Table 2.6. For each substream (corresponding to replica values 0, 1 and 2), we create a sequence of three random variables. The "count" variable is assigned the number of RVs that we create using the "test" for each substream and generator. The sequences generated by each random generator are independent, and for each random generator, the sequences generated by a different substream (i in the example) are also independent.

Listing 2.6: Testing Pareto distributed random variables with different seeds.

```
## Simple example demonstrating use of the RandomVariable class from tcl
set count 3
set rng1 [new RNG]
set rng2 [new RNG]

for {set i 0} {$i<3} {incr i} {
    puts "===== i = $i "
    for {set j 0} {$j < $i} {incr j} {
      $rng1 next-substream;
      $rng2 next-substream;
    }
        set r1 [new RandomVariable/Pareto]
        $r1 use-rng $rng1
```

```
$r1 set avg_ 10.0
$r1 set shape_ 1.2
puts stdout "(rng1) Testing Pareto Distribution , avg = [$r1 set avg_]
   shape = [$r1 set shape_]"
$r1 test $count

set r2 [new RandomVariable/Pareto]
$r2 use-rng $rng2
$r2 set avg_ 10.0
$r2 set shape_ 1.2
puts stdout "(rng2) Testing Pareto Distribution , avg = [$r2 set avg_]
  shape = [$r2 set shape_]"
$r2 test $count
}
```

CHAPTER 3

How to work with trace files

The NS-2 simulator can provide a lot of detailed data on events that occur at the network. If we wish to analyze the data, we may need to extract relevant information from traces and to manipulate them.

One can of course write programs in any programming language that can handle data files.

Yet several tools that seem particularly well adapted for these purposes already exist and are freely available under various operating systems (linux, windows, etc.) All they require is to write short scripts that are interpreted and executed without need for compilation.

3.1 PROCESSING DATA FILES WITH AWK

The awk tool [1] allows us to do simple operations on data files such as averaging the values of a given column, summing or multiplying term by term between several columns, all data-reformatting tasks, etc.

In the following two examples we show how to take the average value of a given column in a file, and then to compute the standard deviation.

```
BEGIN { FS = "\t"} { nl++ } { s=s+$4} END {print "average:" s/nl}
```

Table 3.1: awk script for averaging the values in column 4 of a file.

(Note: the "\t" should be used if columns are tabulated. If not then one should replace it by " ".)

```
BEGIN {FS="\t"}{ln++}{d=$4-t}{s2=s2+d*d} END {print "standev:" sqrt(s2/ln)}
```

Table 3.2: awk script for obtaining the standard deviation of column 4 of a file.

To use the first script to compute the average of column four of a file named "Out.ns," we type in UNIX:

```
awk -f Average.awk Out.ns
```

We shall get as a result something like: `average : 29.397` for the average of column 4 (where the first column is considered as number 1).

To compute now the standard deviation of that column, we type

```
awk -v t=29.397 -f StDev.awk Out.ns
```

which will give in response something like `standev : 33.2003` Note that in the above script, we have to copy the average value obtained from the previous script into the command that computes the standard deviation. This example shows how to pass parameters to an awk script.

Note that if we do not divide at the end of the first awk script (Table 3.1) by nl, we shall obtain simply the sum of entries of column 4 instead of their average.

A recommended way to obtain the average and the standard deviation is using arrays:

```
BEGIN { FS = "\t"} {val[nl]=$4} { nl++ } {s=s+$4} END {
  av=s/nl
  for (i in val) {
    d=val[i]-av
    s2=s2+d*d
  }
  print "average: " av " standev " sqrt(s2/nl)}
```

Table 3.3: Average and Standard Deviation awk script.

The next example takes as input a file with 15 columns (0 to 14). It then creates as output 5 columns, where the first contains column no. 1 of the original file, and columns 2 to 5 are the sum of columns 3-4, 6-8, 9-11 and 12-14, respectively (12-14 correspond to the three last columns in the original file).

```
BEGIN {FS="\t"}{l1=$3+$4+$5}{l2=$6+$7+$8}{d1=$9+$10+$11} \
{d2=$12+$13+$14}{print $1"\t" l1"\t" l2"\t" d1"\t" d2 } END {}
```

Table 3.4: A cut and paste columns awk script.

The use of this script could be as follows:

```
awk -f suma.awk Conn4.tr > outfile
```

The original file here is `Conn4.tr` and the output is written into a file called `outfile`.

3.2   USING GREP

The `grep` command in UNIX allows us to "filter" a file. We can create a new file which consists of only those lines from the original file that contain a given character sequence. For example, output traces in `ns` may contain all types of packets that go through all links, and we may be interested only in the data concerning tcp packets that went from node 0 to node 2. If lines concerning such events contain the string " 0 2 tcp ", then all we have to do is type

```
grep " 0 2 tcp " tr1.tr > tr2.tr
```

where "tr1.tr" is the original trace and "tr2.tr" is the new file. If we wish to obtain a file containing all lines of tr1.tr that begin with the letter r, we should type

```
grep "^r" tr1.tr > tr2.tr
```

If we wish to make a file of all the lines that begin with "s" and have later "tcp 1020", we should type

```
grep "^s" simple.tr | grep "tcp 1020" > tr3.tr
```

3.3   PROCESSING DATA FILES WITH PERL

PERL stands for "Practical Extraction and Report Language". Perl[4] allows easy filtering and processing of ASCII data files in UNIX. This language was created by Larry Wall with the main idea of simplifying the task of system administration. Perl has evolved considerably and nowadays is a general purpose language and one of the most widely used tools for web and Internet data managing.

Perl is an interpreted language which has many uses, but is mainly addressed to search, extraction and report. Some advantages of Perl are:

- Ease implementation of small programs to be used as filters, for extracting information from text files.

- It can be used in many OSs without changing the code.

- Maintaining and debugging of Perl scripts are simpler than programs in other specific languages.

- Perl is very popular, so there exist many of gnu scripts on the web.

We present in this Section some useful Perl scripts.

The first example given in Listing 3.1 computes dynamically the throughput of TCP connections. The program averages the throughput over periods defined by a parameter called "granularity". As input it takes three arguments: the name of a trace file (e.g., out.tr), the node at which we wish to check the throughput of TCP, and the granularity.

Listing 3.1: Perl program for computing throughput.

```perl
# type: perl throughput.pl <trace file> <required node> <granularity>  >   file
$infile=$ARGV[0];
$tonode=$ARGV[1];
$granularity=$ARGV[2];


#we compute how many bytes were transmitted during time interval specified
#by granularity parameter in seconds
$sum=0;
$clock=0;
      open (DATA,"<$infile")
        || die "Can't␣open␣$infile␣$!";

    while (<DATA>) {
            @x = split('␣');

#column 1 is time
if ($x[1]-$clock <= $granularity)
{
#checking if the event corresponds to a reception
if ($x[0] eq 'r')
{
#checking if the destination corresponds to 1st argument
if ($x[3] eq $tonode)
{
#checking if the packet type is TCP
if ($x[4] eq 'tcp')
{
    $sum=$sum+$x[5];
}
}
}
}
else
{   $throughput=$sum/$granularity;
    print STDOUT "$x[1]␣$throughput\n";
    $clock=$clock+$granularity;
    $sum=0;
}
}
    $throughput=$sum/$granularity;
```

```
      print STDOUT "$x[1]␣$throughput\n";
      $clock=$clock+$granularity;
      $sum=0;
      close DATA;
exit(0);
```

3.4   PLOTTING WITH GNUPLOT

Gnuplot is a widely available free software both for UNIX/linux as well as windows operating systems.

Gnuplot has a help command that can be used to learn details of its operation.

The simplest way to use gnuplot is to type "plot $< fn >$", where the file (whose name we write as fn) has two columns representing the x and y values of points. Points can be joined by a line of different styles by writing commands like:

```
plot 'fn' w lines 1
```

(different numbers can be given instead of "1") that produce different line styles). Alternatively, one may use different type of points by writing commands of the form

```
plot 'fn' w points 9
```

(again, several types of points can be depicted depending on the number that appears after "points").

Some other features of gnuplot: consider, for example, the following commands:

```
set size 0.6,0.6
set pointsize 3
set key 100,8
set xrange [90.0:120.0]
plot 'fn1' w lines 1, 'fn2' w lines 8, 'fn3' with points 9
```

- Line 1 will produce a smaller size curve than the default.

- Line 2 will produce points that are larger than the defaults. (In both lines, other numbers can be used).

- Line 3 tells gnuplot where exactly to put the 'key'; the key is the legend part in the figure describing the plotted objects. In particular, it gives for each plotted object the line type or point type that is used. Instead of an exact position, one could use the keywords 'left', 'right', 'top', 'bottom', 'outside' and 'below', e.g., set key below (which sets the key below the graph), or simply "set nokey" which disables the key completely. Note that the default name of each object that appears in the key is simply its corresponding file name. If we wish to give an object a title other than the file name, we have to state this explicitly in the "plot" command, for example:

```
plot 'fn1' t "expectation" w lines 1, 'fn2' t "variance" w lines 2
```

Here, the names "expectation" and "variance" will appear in the key.

- Line 4 restricts the range of the x axis to the interval 90-120.

- Line 5 superimposes three curves in a single figure, obtained from three different files: fn1, fn2, fn3.

If the same sequence of commands are to be used several times, one can write them into a file, say having the name "g1.com", and then simply load the file each time one wishes to use it:

```
load 'g1.com'
```

gnuplot can be used to extract some column from a multicolumn file. This is done as follows

```
plot 'queue.tr' using 1:($4/1000) t "kbytes" w lines 1, \
     'queue.tr' using 1:5 t "packets" w lines 2
```

which means plotting first a curve using column 1 of the file "queue.tr' as the x axis and 4 divided by 1000 as the y axis, and then plotting on the same curve the column 5 for the y axis using the same column 1 for the x axis. Note: this order between "using", "t" and "lines" is important!

3.5   PLOTTING WITH XGRAPH

Xgraph is a plotting utility that is provided by NS-2. (Sometimes it needs separate compiling using ./configure and then make when at the directory xgraph. Also, sometimes this does not work with the xgraph that arrives with the whole NS-2 single package, and it can then be downloaded and installed separately). Note that it allows to create postscript, Tgif files, and others, by clicking on the button "Hdcpy". It can be invoked within the tcl command which thus results in an immediate display at the end of the simulation.

As input, the xgraph command expects one or more ascii files containing each $x - y$ data point pair perl line. For example, xgraph f1 f2 will print on the same figure the files f1 and f2.

Some options in xgraph are:

- Title: use -t "title".

- Size: -geometry xsize x ysize.

- Title for axis: -x "xtitle" (for the title of the x axis) and -y "ytitle" (for the title of the y axis).

- Color of text and grid: with the flag -v.

An example of a command would be

```
xgraph f1 f2 -geometry 800x400 -t "Loss rates" -x "time" -y "Lost packets"
```

3.6 EXTRACTING INFORMATION WITHIN A TCL SCRIPT

It is possible to integrate UNIX commands such as "grep" and "awk" already into the tcl scripts, so as to start the processing of data while writing the file. For example, another way to limit the tracing files (or in general, to process them online while they are being written) is to use linux commands related to file processing within the tcl command that opens the required file.

For example, we may replace the command $set file1 [open out.tr w] (that we had at the beginning of the script ex1.tcl, see Listing 2.4) by the command

```
set file1 [open "| grep \"tcp\" > out.tr" w]
```

This will result in filtering the lines written to the file "out.tr" and leaving only those that contain the word "tcp".

CHAPTER 4

Description and simulation of TCP/IP

TCP (*Transport Control Protocol*) is the transport protocol that is responsible for the transmission of around 90% of the Internet traffic, and understanding TCP is thus crucial for dimensioning the Internet. Although TCP is already largely deployed, it continues to evolve.

In the first section we describe the operation of TCP. Then in subsequent sections we present several NS-2 scripts that illustrate the analysis of TCP through simulations.

4.1   DESCRIPTION OF TCP

4.1.1   OBJECTIVES OF TCP AND WINDOW FLOW CONTROL

TCP has several objectives:

- Adapt the transmission rate of packets to the available bandwidth,

- Avoid congestion at the network, and

- Create a reliable connection by retransmitting lost packets.

In order to control the transmission rate, the number of packets that have not yet been received (or more precisely, for which the source has not obtained the information of good reception) is bounded by a parameter called a congestion window. We denote it by W, but it is called *cwnd* in the TCP code. This means that the source is obliged to wait and stop transmission whenever the number of packets that it has transmitted and that have not been "acknowledged" reaches W. In order to acknowledge packets and thus to be able to retransmit lost packets, each transmitted packet has a sequence number.

4.1.2   ACKNOWLEDGEMENTS

The objectives of Acknowledgements (ACKs) are:

- Regulate the transmission rate of TCP, ensuring that packets can be transmitted only when others have left the network.

- Render the connection reliable by transmitting to the source information it needs so as to retransmit packets that have not reached the destination.

How does the destination know that a packet is missing?

How do we know that a packet is lost?

What information does the ACK carry along?

The ACK tells the source what is the sequence number of the packet it expects. This is illustrated by the following example. Suppose packets 1,2,...,6 have reached the destination (in order). When packet 6 arrives, the destination sends an ACK to say it expects packet number 7. If packet 7 arrives, the destination requests number 8. Suppose packet 8 is lost and packet 9 arrives well. At that time, the destination sends an ACK called "repeated ACK" as it tells the source that it awaits packet 8. The information carried by the ACK is thus the same as the one carried by the previous ACK.

This method is called "implicit ACK". It is robust under losses of ACKs. Indeed, assume that the ACK saying that the destination waits for packet 5 is lost. When the next ACK arrives, saying it awaits packet 6, the source knows that the destination has received packet 5, so the information sent by the lost ACK is deduced from the next ACK.

A TCP packet is considered lost if

- Three repeated ACKs for the same packet arrive at the source[1], or

- When a packet is transmitted, there is a timer that starts counting. If its ACK does not arrive within a period T_0, there is a "Time-Out" and the packet is considered to be lost.

Retransmitting after three duplicated ACKS is called "fast retransmit".

How to choose T_0? The source has an estimation of the average round trip time RTT, which is the time necessary for a packet to reach the destination plus the time for its ACK to reach the source. It also has an estimation of the variability of RTT. T_0 is determined as follows:

$$T_0 = \overline{RTT} + 4D$$

Where $\overline{RTT}$ is the current estimation of RTT, and D is the estimation of the variability of RTT. In order to estimate RTT, we measure the difference M between the transmission time of a packet and the time its ACK returns. Then we compute

$$\overline{RTT} \leftarrow a \times \overline{RTT} + (1-a)M,$$

$$D \leftarrow aD + (1-a)|\overline{RTT} - M|.$$

In order to decrease the number of ACKs in the system, TCP frequently uses the "delayed ACK" option where an ACK is transmitted only for every d packets that reach the destination. The standard value of d is 2. However, delaying an ACK till $d > 1$ packets are received could result in a deadlock in case the window size is one. Therefore, if the first packet (of an expected group of d

---

[1]One does not consider a single repeated ACK as a loss indication since duplicated ACKS could be due to resequencing of packets at the Internet.

packets) arrives at the destination, then after some time interval (typically 100ms) if d packets have not yet arrived, then an acknowledgement is generated without further waiting.

4.1.3   DYNAMIC CONGESTION WINDOW

Since the beginning of the eighties, for several years, TCP had a fixed congestion window. Networks at that time were unstable, there were many losses, large and severe congestion periods, during which the throughputs decreased substantially, there were many packet retransmissions and large delays. In order to solve this problem, Van Jacobson [37] proposed to use a dynamic congestion window: its size can vary according to the network state. The basic idea is as follows: When the window is small, it can grow rapidly, and when it reaches large values it can only grow slowly. When congestion is detected, the window size decreases drastically. This dynamic mechanism allows to resolve congestion rapidly and yet use efficiently the network's bandwidth.

More precisely, define a threshold W_{th} called "slow start threshold" which represents our estimation of the network capacity. The window starts at a value of one. It thus transmits a single packet. When its ACK returns, we can transmit two packets. For each ACK of these two packets, the window increases by one, so that when the ACKs of these two packets return we transmit four packets. We see that there is an exponential growth of the window. This phase is called "slow start". It is so called because in spite of the rapid growth, it is slower than if we had started directly with a value of $W = W_{th}$.

When $W = W_{th}$, we pass to a second phase called "congestion avoidance", where the window W increases by $\lfloor 1/W \rfloor$ with each ACK that returns. After transmitting W packets, W increases by 1. If we transmit the W packets at t, then at time $t + RTT$ we transmit $W + 1$, and at $t + 2RTT$ we transmit $W + 2$, etc. We see that the window growth is linear.

4.1.4   LOSSES AND A DYNAMIC THRESHOLD W_{th}

Not only is W dynamic, W_{th} is too. It is fixed in TCP to half the value of W when there has been a packet loss.

There are several variants of TCP. In the first variant, called "Tahoe", whenever a loss is detected then the window reduces to the value of 1 and a slow-start phase begins. This is a drastic decrease of the window size and thus of the transmission rate.

In the other mostly used variants, called Reno or New-Reno, the window drops to 1 only if the loss is detected through a time-out. When a loss is detected through repeated ACKs then the congestion window drops by half. Slow start is not initiated and we remain in the "congestion avoidance" phase.

4.1.5   INITIATING A CONNECTION

To initiate a TCP connection, the source sends a "sync" packet of 40 bytes to the destination. The destination then sends an ACK (also 40 packets long, called "sync ACK"). When receiving this

ACK, TCP can start sending data. Note that: if either of these packets is lost then after a time-out expires (usually 3 or 6 secs) it is retransmitted. When a retransmitted packet is lost, the time-out duration doubles and the packet is sent again.

4.2   TRACING AND ANALYSIS OF EXAMPLE EX1.TCL

Let us run the perl program "throughput.pl" (Table 3.1) on the trace file out.tr generated by the ex1.tcl script (see Table 2.4). We have to type:

```
perl throughput.pl out.tr 4 1 > thp
```

We obtain an output file with the averaged received throughput of TCP (in bytes per second) as a function of time, where in our case, each 1 second, a new value of the throughput is obtained. This output file can be displayed using gnuplot by typing:

```
gnuplot
set size 0.4,0.4
set key 60,15000
plot 'thp' w lines 1
```

The result is given in Figure 4.1.

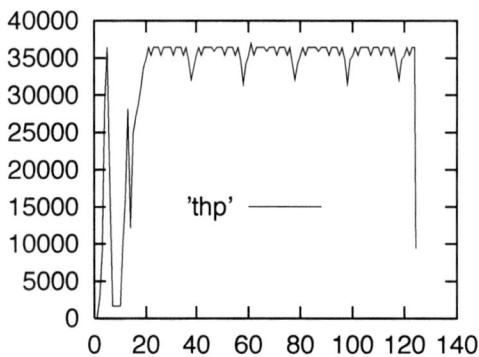

Figure 4.1: Throughput of TCP connection.   Figure 4.2: Window size of TCP connection.

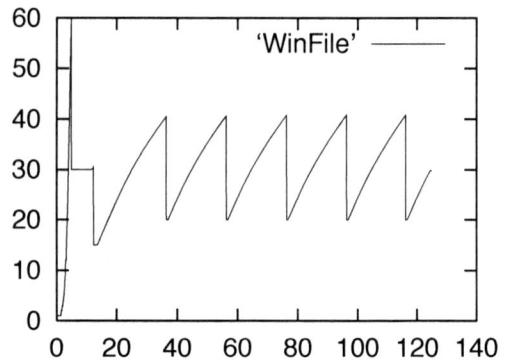

In order to understand better the behavior of the system, we also plot the window size (Figure 4.2). This is the file "WinFile" created by running ex1.tcl.

We see that from time 20 onwards a steady-state cyclic regime of TCP is attained: TCP is always in congestion avoidance, and its window size increases (almost linearly) until congestion occurs.

Before time 20, we see a transient behavior in which TCP is in the slow-start phase.

At time 4.2 there are losses at the slow start phase. The window halves, whereas the throughput becomes close to zero. How can we explain that? The reason is that at time 4.2 there is a time-out, so although the window is of size 30 (packets), there are no transmissions. At time 11 there are again losses during a slow-start phase.

4.3   TCP OVER NOISY LINKS AND QUEUE MONITORING

In the previous examples losses were due to congestion. In practice, losses may also be caused by noisy links. This is especially true in the case of radio links, e.g., in cellular phones or in satellite links. A link may become, in fact, completely disconnected for some period. We shall see this aspect later, in Section 5.1. Or it may suffer from occasional interference (due to shadowing, fading, etc.) that causes packets to contain errors and then to be dropped. In this section we shall show how to introduce the simplest error model: we assume that packets are dropped on the *forward* link with some fixed constant probability.

This link error model, which will be introduced to the link connecting nodes n3 and n2 (in the example in Figure 4.3), is created as follows:

```
#Set error model on link n2 to n3.
set loss_module [new ErrorModel]
$loss_module set rate_ 0.2
$loss_module ranvar [new RandomVariable/Uniform]
$loss_module drop-target [new Agent/Null]
$ns lossmodel $loss_module $n2 $n3
```

The command $loss_module set rate_ 0.2 determines a loss rate of 20% of the packets. It uses a generator of a uniformly distributed random variable, which is declared in the next line. The last line determines which link will be affected.

As an example of a TCP connection that shares a noisy bottleneck link with a UDP connection, we consider the network depicted in Figure 4.3.

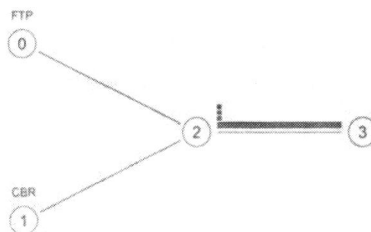

Figure 4.3: Example rdrop.tcl.

Queue monitoring   An important object of NS-2 is the monitor-queue. It allows to collect much useful information on queue length, on the arrivals, departures and losses. To implement a queue monitor between nodes n2 and n3, we type:

```
set qmon [$ns monitor-queue $n2 $n3 [open qm.out w] 0.1];
[$ns link $n2 $n3] queue-sample-timeout; # [$ns link $n2 $n3] start-tracing
```

The "monitor-queue" object has 4 arguments: the first two defines the link where the queue is located, the third is the output trace file and the last says how frequently we wish to monitor the queue. In our case, the queue at the input of node n2-n3 is monitored every 0.1 sec and the output is printed into the file qm.out. Note that you can use either of the two methods ("queue-sample-timeout" or "start-tracing") in order to start the queue monitor.

The output file contains the following 11 columns:

- the time,

- the input and output nodes defining the queue,

- the queue size in bytes (corresponds to the attribute size_ of the monitor-queue object),

- the queue size in packets, (corresponds to the attribute pkt_),

- the number of packets that have arrived, (corresponds to the attribute parrivals_),

- the number of packets that have departed the link, (corresponds to the attribute pdepartures_),

- the number of packets dropped at the queue, (corresponds to the attribute pdrops_),

- the number of bytes that have arrived, (corresponds to the attribute barrivals_),

- the number of bytes that have departed the link, (corresponds to the attribute bdepartures_),

- the number of bytes dropped (corresponds to the attribute bdrops_).

An alternative way to work directly with these attributes is described in Section 4.5.

Listing 4.1 shows the entire script for modelling TCP with noisy drops.

Listing 4.1: Tcl script rdrop.tcl for TCP over a noisy channel.

```
set ns [new Simulator]          # Create the simulator instance
$ns color 1 Blue
$ns color 2 Red


set nf [open out.nam w]         #Open the NAM trace file
$ns namtrace-all $nf


set tf [open out.tr w]          #Open the Trace file
set windowVsTime2 [open WindowVsTimeNReno w]
$ns trace-all $tf
```

```
proc finish {} {                       #Define a 'finish' procedure
        global ns nf tf
        $ns flush-trace
        close $nf
        close $tf
        exec nam out.nam &
        exit 0
}
set n0 [$ns node]                   #Create four nodes
set n1 [$ns node]
set n2 [$ns node]
set n3 [$ns node]


$ns at 0.1 "$n1 label \"CBR\""
$ns at 1.0 "$n0 label \"FTP\""


#Create links between the nodes
$ns duplex-link $n0 $n2 2Mb 10ms DropTail
$ns duplex-link $n1 $n2 2Mb 10ms DropTail
$ns simplex-link $n2 $n3 0.07Mb 20ms DropTail
$ns simplex-link $n3 $n2 0.07Mb 20ms DropTail


#Set Queue Size of link (n2-n3) to 10
$ns queue-limit $n2 $n3 10


#Monitor the queue for link (n2-n3). (for NAM)
$ns simplex-link-op $n2 $n3 queuePos 0.5


#Set error model on link n3 to n2.
set loss_module [new ErrorModel]
$loss_module set rate_ 0.2
$loss_module ranvar [new RandomVariable/Uniform]
$loss_module drop-target [new Agent/Null]
$ns lossmodel $loss_module $n2 $n3


#Setup a TCP connection
set tcp [new Agent/TCP/Newreno]
$ns attach-agent $n0 $tcp
set sink [new Agent/TCPSink/DelAck]
$ns attach-agent $n3 $sink
$ns connect $tcp $sink
```

```
$tcp set fid_ 1

#Setup a FTP over TCP connection
set ftp [new Application/FTP]
$ftp attach-agent $tcp
$ftp set type_ FTP

#Setup a UDP connection
set udp [new Agent/UDP]
$ns attach-agent $n1 $udp
set null [new Agent/Null]
$ns attach-agent $n3 $null
$ns connect $udp $null
$udp set fid_ 2

#Setup a CBR over UDP connection
set cbr [new Application/Traffic/CBR]
$cbr attach-agent $udp
$cbr set type_ CBR
$cbr set packetSize_ 1000
$cbr set rate_ 0.01Mb
$cbr set random_ false

#Schedule events for the CBR and FTP agents
$ns at 0.1 "$cbr start"
$ns at 1.0 "$ftp start"
$ns at 624.0 "$ftp stop"
$ns at 624.5 "$cbr stop"

# Printing the window size
proc plotWindow {tcpSource file} {
global ns
set time 0.01
set now [$ns now]
set cwnd [$tcpSource set cwnd_]
puts $file "$now $cwnd"
$ns at [expr $now+$time] "plotWindow $tcpSource $file" }
$ns at 1.1 "plotWindow $tcp $windowVsTime2"

# sample the bottleneck queue every 0.1 sec. store the trace in qm.out
set qmon [$ns monitor-queue $n2 $n3 [open qm.out w] 0.1];
[$ns link $n2 $n3] queue-sample-timeout; # [$ns link $n2 $n3] start-tracing
```

```
#Detach tcp and sink agents (not really necessary)
$ns at 624.5 "$ns detach-agent $n0 $tcp ; $ns detach-agent $n3 $sink"


$ns at 625.0 "finish"
$ns run
```

In Figure 4.4 we trace (using gnuplot) the file WindowVsTimeNReno created by the simulation. A zoomed version is given in Figure 4.5.

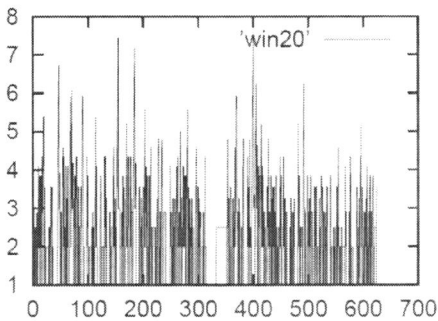

Figure 4.4: Window size of TCP with 20% random losses.

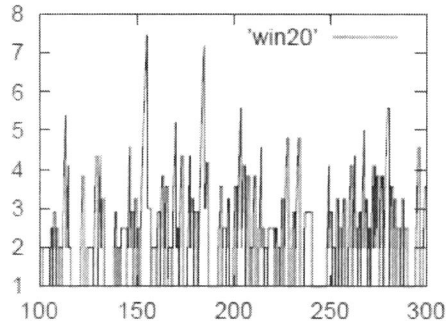

Figure 4.5: Window size of TCP with 20% random losses: a zoom.

In several cases we can observe long timeouts, in particular at time 300. To see the huge impact of the random loss on TCP performance, we run the simulation again but with no losses. The result is depicted in Figure 4.6.

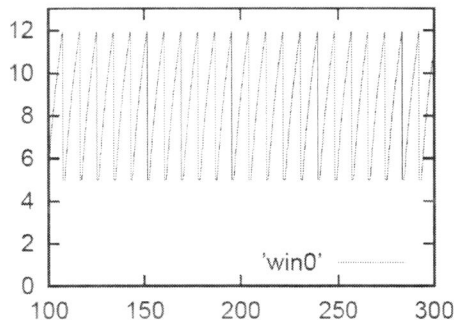

Figure 4.6: TCP window size for 0 random loss rate.

An important performance measure is the average throughput of TCP. A very simple way to compute it is to search in the trace file out.tr the time that a TCP packet was received at the destination (at node 3). In our simulation this is found at time 624.08754 and the corresponding trace line is

```
r 624.082754 2 3 tcp 1000 ------- 1 0.0 3.0 1562 4350
```

The number before the last means that this is the 1562*nd* TCP packet to be well received at the destination. The TCP throughput is thus simply this number divided by the duration of the FTP connection (623 seconds), i.e., 2.507 packets per second, or equivalently, 2.507 Kbytes per second (as a TCP packet contains by default 1000 bytes) or 20058 bps.

Note: if we look at the first lines of the out.tr file, we shall see that there are other TCP packets (of size 40 packets each) which we have not been counted in the total number 1562. Their serial number is zero. We do not count them because they correspond to *signalling* packets that are involved in the opening of the TCP connection.

Note that we used the delayed Ack version of TCP by using the command   set sink [new Agent/TCPSink/DelAck]   instead of   simply set sink [new Agent/TCPSink].

4.4   CREATING MANY CONNECTIONS WITH RANDOM FEATURES

In order to create many connections, it is useful instead of defining each node, link, connection or application individually to define them as vectors (or arrays) in tcl (within loop statements).

Furthermore, it becomes of interest to choose connection parameters (such as time of beginning or end of activity, link delays, etc.) in a random way. We treat both issues in this Section, and then provide an example. Note that we have already considered other aspects of randomness in Section 4.3.

Example 4.1   An example. Consider the network at Figure 4.7. The tcl script is given in Listing

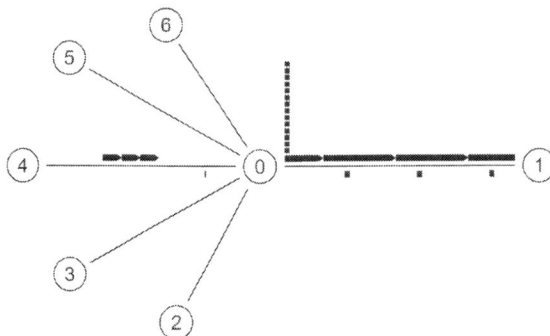

Figure 4.7: Example of a network with several TCP connections.

4.2.

We create 5 FTP connections that start at random: the starting time is uniformly distributed between 0 and 7 sec. The whole simulation duration is 10 seconds. We create links with delay that is chosen at random, uniformly distributed between 1ms and 5ms.

In addition to the standard trace outputs, we also create a file named "win" that will contain the evolution of the window size of all connections at a granularity of 0.03sec. This is done in the procedure plotWindow. Note that the file "win" is addressed using the pointer "windowVsTimes". The procedure is called recursively for each of the 5 connections.

Listing 4.2: Tcl script ex3.tcl for several competing TCP connections.

```
set ns [new Simulator]              #Create the simulator instance
set nf [open out.nam w]             #Opening the trace files
$ns namtrace-all $nf
set tf [open out.tr w]
set windowVsTime [open win w]
set param [open parameters w]
$ns trace-all $tf

proc finish {} {                    #Define a 'finish' procedure
        global ns nf tf
        $ns flush-trace
        close $nf
        close $tf
        exec nam out.nam &
        exit 0
}
#Create bottleneck and destination nodes and link between them
set n2 [$ns node]
set n3 [$ns node]
$ns duplex-link $n2 $n3 0.7Mb 20ms DropTail

set NumbSrc 5
set Duration 10

for {set j 1} {$j<=$NumbSrc} { incr j } {          #Source nodes
set S($j) [$ns node]
}

# Create a random generator for starting the ftp and for bottleneck link delays
set rep 1
set rng1 [new RNG]
```

```
set rng2 [new RNG]
for {set i 0} {$i < $rep} {incr i} {
    $rng1 next-substream;
    $rng2 next-substream;
}


# parameters for random variables for delays
set RVdly [new RandomVariable/Uniform]
$RVdly set min_ 1
$RVdly set max_ 5
$RVdly use-rng $rng1

# parameters for random variables for beginning of ftp connections
set RVstart [new RandomVariable/Uniform]
$RVstart set min_ 0
$RVstart set max_ 7
$RVstart use-rng $rng2


#We define two random parameters for each connection
for {set i 1} {$i<=$NumbSrc} { incr i } {
        set startT($i)  [expr [$RVstart value]]
        set dly($i) [expr [$RVdly value]]
        puts $param "dly($i) $dly($i) ms"
        puts $param "startT($i)  $startT($i) sec" }


#Links between source and bottleneck
for {set j 1} {$j<=$NumbSrc} { incr j } {
        $ns duplex-link $S($j) $n2 10Mb $dly($j)ms DropTail
        $ns queue-limit $S($j) $n2 100 }


#Monitor the queue for link (n2-n3). (for NAM)
$ns duplex-link-op $n2 $n3 queuePos 0.5


$ns queue-limit $n2 $n3 10                 #Set Queue Size of link (n2-n3) to 10


for {set j 1} {$j<=$NumbSrc} { incr j } {       #TCP Sources
        set tcp_src($j) [new Agent/TCP/Reno]
}
for {set j 1} {$j<=$NumbSrc} { incr j } {       #TCP Destinations
        set tcp_snk($j) [new Agent/TCPSink]
}
for {set j 1} {$j<=$NumbSrc} { incr j } {       #Connections
```

```
        $ns attach-agent $S($j) $tcp_src($j)
        $ns attach-agent $n3 $tcp_snk($j)
        $ns connect $tcp_src($j) $tcp_snk($j)
}
for {set j 1} {$j<=$NumbSrc} { incr j } {        #FTP sources
        set ftp($j) [$tcp_src($j) attach-source FTP]
}
#Parametrisation of TCP sources
for {set j 1} {$j<=$NumbSrc} { incr j } {
        $tcp_src($j) set packetSize_ 552
}
#Schedule events for the FTP agents:
for {set i 1} {$i<=$NumbSrc} { incr i } {
        $ns at $startT($i) "$ftp($i) start"
        $ns at $Duration "$ftp($i) stop"
}
proc plotWindow {tcpSource file k} {
        global ns

        set time 0.03
        set now [$ns now]
        set cwnd [$tcpSource set cwnd_]
        puts $file "$now $cwnd"
        $ns at [expr $now+$time] "plotWindow $tcpSource $file $k" }

# The procedure will now be called for all tcp sources
for {set j 1} {$j<=$NumbSrc} { incr j } {
        $ns at 0.1 "plotWindow $tcp_src($j) $windowVsTime $j"
}

$ns at [expr $Duration] "finish"
$ns run
```

4.5   SHORT TCP CONNECTIONS

File transfers constitute the majority of the traffic over the Internet. The average transferred file is around 10Kbytes. This means that an "average" file has no more than 10 TCP packets taking the typical TCP packet size to be 1Kbyte [20, 54]. This implies that most of the file transfers end in slow start phase. These files are frequently called "mice". Surprisingly, however, most traffic in the Internet is transmitted by very long files. These are called "elephants". A typical distribution that describes the file size is the Pareto [20], with shape parameter of between 1 and 2 [20] (and average of 10KB).

The median of the file size is around 2.5Kbytes ([54] and references therein). Note that a Pareto distribution with mean 10Kbytes and a median size of 2.5Kbytes defines a Pareto distribution with shape parameter $\beta = 1.16$ and with a minimum size of 1.37Kbytes. The distribution of interarrival times of new connections is frequently taken to be exponential.

In this Section we shall present ways to simulate short sessions, and to measure the distribution of the transmission duration, of the number of ongoing connections and the throughput.

We shall consider a network with the same topology as the one in Figure 4.2: several sources sharing a common bottleneck node and a common destination. The number of sources is given by the parameter "NodeNb" (in our example it is 6). TCP sources are parameterized now by two parameters: the source node and the session number from that node. For each TCP agent we define a new FTP application. New TCP connections arrive according to a Poisson process. We shall therefore generate the beginning of a new TCP connection using exponentially distributed random variables.

The bottleneck link is assumed to be of 2Mbps, to have a delay of 1ms and to have a queue of size 3000. All other input links that join this link have a bandwidth of 100 Mbps and a delay of 1ms. We use the New Reno version with a maximum window size of 2000.

The average time between the arrivals of new TCP sessions at each node is in our example 45 msec. This means that on the average, 22.22 new sessions arrive at each node so that the global arrival rate of sessions is 22.22 times NodeNb, which gives in our case 133.33 sessions/sec. We generate sessions of random size with a mean of 10Kbytes, with Pareto distribution with shape 1.5. The global rate of generation of bits is thus

$$133.33 \times 10^4 \times 8 = 10.67 Mbps.$$

We see that the rate of generation of bits is larger than the bottleneck capacity, so we shall expect a congestion phenomenon to appear. However, TCP has the capacity to avoid congestion in the network (at the bottleneck queue). Congestion will therefore appear in other forms as we shall see.

Monitoring the number of sessions   In the context of short TCP sessions we are interested not only in packet statistics but also in session statistics. In the NS-2 program we shall define a recursive procedure, called "Test", that checks for each session whether it has ended. The procedure calls itself each 0.1 sec (this is set in the variable "time"). If a connection has ended then we print in an output file

- the connection ids i and j (where (i, j) stands for the jth connection from node i),

- the start and end time of that connection,

- the throughput of that connection, and

- the size of the transfer in bytes.

The procedure then defines another beginning of transfer after a random time. In the script that follows, the output file will be Out.ns. To check whether a session has ended, we use the command

`if {[$tcpsrc($i,$j) set ack_]==[$tcpsrc($i,$j) set maxseq_]} {`

Another recursive procedure called "countFlows" is used to update the number of active connections from each node (stored in a vector "Cnts" whose jth element corresponds to the number of ongoing connections from node j.[2] The procedure has two parameters: "ind" and "sign". The "ind" indicates which source node it concerns. The "sign" indicates to the procedure what to do: it is 0 when a call ends and 1 when it begins. These parameters are used when calling the procedure at the beginning or end of a connection. The procedure also calls itself periodically every 0.2 seconds and it then prints the number of active calls into a file (Conn.tr). To do that, the "sign" parameter that is passed should be neither 1 nor 0 (we set it as 3).

Monitoring the queue   In the next tcl program, we present an alternative way to do queue monitoring, more sophisticated than the method we saw in Section 4.3. We use again the commands

`set qfile [$ns monitor-queue $N $D  [open queue.tr w] 0.05]`
`[$ns link $N $D] queue-sample-timeout;`

We could however delete the second line. Instead of restricting ourselves to that command, we work directly with the attributes of the "monitor-queue" which have been described in Section 4.3. This is done in a procedure called "record" that is recursively called every 0.05 sec. For example, we print the used bandwidth of the queue (in Kbytes per second) into a file by dividing the number of departures in a time epoch by the epoch duration. Note that the monitor-queue keeps track of the total number of arrived bytes in the attribute `bdepartures_`. In order to count only the number of departures in a time epoch (and not during the entire simulation duration), we have to reset the value of `bdepartures_` at the end of each new computation of the bandwidth.

Listing 4.3: Tcl script shortTcp.tcl for short TCP connections.

```
set ns [new Simulator]

# There are several sources of TCP sharing a bottleneck link
# and a single destination. Their number is given by the parameter NodeNb
#       S(1)            ----
#        .                |
#        .              ---- ---- N -------- D(1)...D(NodeNb)
#        .                |
#       S(NodeNb)       ----
set Out [open Out.ns w]          # Out.ns file will contain the transfer times
set Conn [open Conn.tr w]        # Next file will contain the number of connections
```

[2]The interest in having different counters at different nodes lies in the fact that we can also use the program for the case of asymmetric input links, in which case we shall be able to study the dependence of the performance on the link delay and bandwidth.

```
set tf [open out.tr w]           # Open the Trace file
$ns trace-all $tf


# We define three files that will be used to trace the queue size, the bandwidth
# and losses at the bottleneck.
set qsize [open queuesize.tr w]
set qbw   [open queuebw.tr   w]
set qlost [open queuelost.tr w]


# defining the topology
set N [$ns node]
set D [$ns node]
$ns duplex-link $N $D 2Mb 1ms DropTail
$ns queue-limit $N $D 3000


set NodeNb 6           # Number of sources
set NumberFlows 530    # Number of flows per source node

for {set j 1} {$j<=$NodeNb} { incr j } {         #Nodes and links
        set S($j) [$ns node]
        $ns duplex-link $S($j) $N 100Mb 1ms DropTail
        $ns queue-limit $S($j) $N 1000
}
for {set i 1} {$i<=$NodeNb} { incr i } {         #TCP Sources and Destinations
        for {set j 1} {$j<=$NumberFlows} { incr j } {
                set tcpsrc($i,$j) [new Agent/TCP/Newreno]
                set tcp_snk($i,$j) [new Agent/TCPSink]
                $tcpsrc($i,$j) set window_ 2000
        }
}
for {set i 1} {$i<=$NodeNb} { incr i } {         #Connections
        for {set j 1} {$j<=$NumberFlows} { incr j } {
                $ns attach-agent $S($i) $tcpsrc($i,$j)
                $ns attach-agent $D $tcp_snk($i,$j)
                $ns connect $tcpsrc($i,$j) $tcp_snk($i,$j)
        }
}
for {set i 1} {$i<=$NodeNb} { incr i } {         #FTP sources
        for {set j 1} {$j<=$NumberFlows} { incr j } {
                set ftp($i,$j) [$tcpsrc($i,$j) attach-source FTP]
        }
}
```

```
# Generators for random size of files and interarrivals.
set rep 1
set rng1 [new RNG]
set rng2 [new RNG]
for {set i 0} {$i < $rep} {incr i} {
$rng1 next-substream;
$rng2 next-substream;
}
# Random interarrival time of TCP transfers at each source i
set RV [new RandomVariable/Exponential]
$RV set avg_ 0.045
$RV use-rng $rng1

# Random size of files to transmit
set RVSize [new RandomVariable/Pareto]
$RVSize set avg_ 10000
$RVSize set shape_ 1.5  \cite{Jacob}
$RVSize use-rng $rng2

# We now define the beginning times of transfers and the transfer sizes
# Arrivals of sessions follow a Poisson process.
for {set i 1} {$i<=$NodeNb} { incr i } {
    set t [$ns now]
    for {set j 1} {$j<=$NumberFlows} { incr j } {
        # set the beginning time of next transfer from source i
        set t [expr $t + [$RV value]]
        set Conct($i,$j) $t

        # set the size of next transfer from source i
        set Size($i,$j) [expr [$RVSize value]]
        $ns at $Conct($i,$j) "$ftp($i,$j) send $Size($i,$j)"

        # update the number of flows
        $ns at $Conct($i,$j) "countFlows $i 1"
} }
# Next is a recursive procedure that checks for each session whether
# it has ended. The procedure calls itself each 0.1 sec (this is
# set in the variable "time").
# If a connection has ended then we print in the file $Out
#    * the connection identifiers i and j,
#    * the start and end time of the connection,
#    * the throughput of the session,
```

```
#     * the size of the transfer in bytes
# and we further define another beginning of transfer after a random time.
proc Test {} {
        global Conct tcpsrc Size NodeNb NumberFlows ns RV ftp Out tcp_snk RVSize
        set time 0.1
        for {set i 1} {$i<=$NodeNb} { incr i } {
                for {set j 1} {$j<=$NumberFlows} { incr j } {

                # We now check if the transfer is over
                 if {[$tcpsrc($i,$j) set ack_]==[$tcpsrc($i,$j) set maxseq_]} {
                  if {[$tcpsrc($i,$j) set ack_]>=0} {
                # If the transfer is over, we print relevant information in $Out
                        puts $Out "$i,$j\t$Conct($i,$j)\t[expr [$ns now]]\t\
   [expr ($Size($i,$j))/(1000*([expr [$ns now]] - $Conct($i,$j)))]\t$Size($i,$j)"
                        countFlows $i 0
                        $tcpsrc($i,$j)  reset
                        $tcp_snk($i,$j) reset
} } } }
$ns at [expr [$ns now]+$time] "Test"
}
for {set j 1} {$j<=$NodeNb} { incr j } {
        set Cnts($j) 0
}
# The following recursive procedure updates the number of connections
# as a function of time. Each 0.2 it prints them into $Conn. This
# is done by calling the procedure with the "sign" parameter equal
# 3 (in which case the "ind" parameter does not play a role). The
# procedure is also called by the Test procedure whenever a connection
# from source i ends by assigning the "sign" parameter 0, or when
# it begins, by assigning it 1 (i is passed through the "ind" variable).
proc countFlows { ind sign } {
        global Cnts Conn NodeNb
        set ns [Simulator instance]

        if { $sign==0 } { set Cnts($ind) [expr $Cnts($ind) - 1]
        } elsif { $sign==1 } { set Cnts($ind) [expr $Cnts($ind) + 1]
        } else {
                puts -nonewline $Conn "[$ns now] \t"
                set sum 0
                for {set j 1} {$j<=$NodeNb} { incr j } {
                        puts -nonewline $Conn "$Cnts($j) \t"
                        set sum [expr $sum + $Cnts($j)]
```

```
                }
                puts $Conn "$sum"
                $ns at [expr [$ns now] + 0.2] "countFlows 1 3"
        }}
proc finish {} {                    #Define a 'finish' procedure
        global ns tf qsize qbw qlost
        $ns flush-trace
        close $qsize
        close $qbw
        close $qlost
# Execute xgraph to display the queue size, queue bandwidth and loss rate
exec xgraph queuesize.tr -geometry 800x400 -t "Queue size" -x "secs" -y "# packs" &
exec xgraph queuebw.tr -geometry 800x400 -t "bandwidth" -x "secs" -y "Kbps" &
exec xgraph queuelost.tr -geometry 800x400 -t "# Packs lost" -x "secs" -y "packs" &
        exit 0
}
# QUEUE MONiTORiNG
set qfile [$ns monitor-queue $N $D  [open queue.tr w] 0.05]
[$ns link $N $D] queue-sample-timeout;

# The following procedure records queue size, bandwidth and loss rate
proc record {} {
        global ns qfile qsize qbw qlost N D
        set time 0.05
        set now [$ns now]
# print the current queue size in $qsize, the current used
# bandwidth in $qbw, and the loss rate in $qloss
        $qfile instvar parrivals_ pdepartures_ bdrops_ bdepartures_ pdrops_
        puts $qsize "$now [expr $parrivals_-$pdepartures_-$pdrops_]"
        puts $qbw   "$now [expr $bdepartures_*8/1024/$time]"
        set bdepartures_ 0
        puts $qlost "$now [expr $pdrops_/$time]"
        $ns at [expr $now+$time] "record"
}


$ns at 0.0 "record"
$ns at 0.01 "Test"
$ns at 0.5 "countFlows 1 3"
$ns at 20 "finish"
$ns run
```

The number of sessions generated (530 per source) ensured that arrivals from all nodes continued till the end of the simulations.

When running the script we obtain the queue size in Kbytes and in packets as depicted in Figure 4.8.

We also ran later the simulation with a reduced number of 130 sessions per node, and the queue size in Kbytes and in packets as depicted in Figure 4.9.

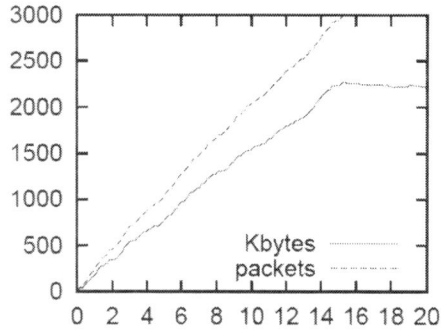

Figure 4.8: Queue size for the example in shortTcp.tcl.

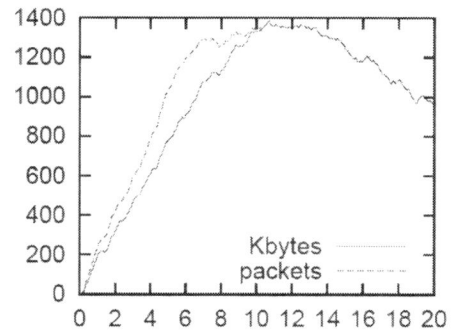

Figure 4.9: Queue size for the example in shortTcp.tcl where we limit the number of sessions.

Here are some observations:

1. In both figures, the number of packets at the queue is larger than the number of Kbytes queued. This may seem strange since a TCP packet has a size of 1Kbyte! The reason is that a very large number of sessions are very small (3 packets or less). Therefore the number of overhead packets of size 40 bytes (that are sent at the beginning of each TCP connection) is considerable (around one out of three!). Taking into account these short packets as well, there are more packets than Kbytes.

2. Observe that in Figure 4.8 the queue size stabilizes at 3000; this is the maximum queue size that is reached. From this moment on there will be losses at the queue.

3. Whereas the number of packets is always larger than the number of Kbytes queued in Figure 4.8, we see that in Figure 4.9 after some time, the number of packets agrees with the number of Kbytes. At this point all packets at the queue are TCP data packets and there are no packets of 40 bytes corresponding to beginning of sessions. This is due to the fact that we limited the number of sessions per node to 130.

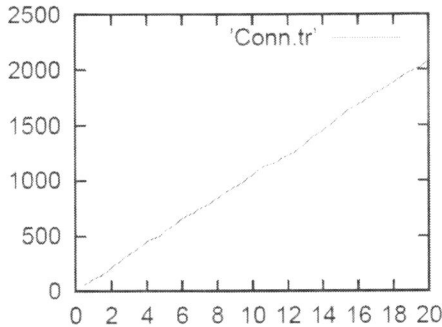

Figure 4.10: Number of Connections.

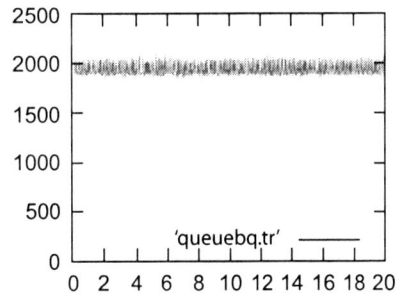

Figure 4.11: Used bandwidth at the bottleneck.

4. If we subtract the output rate of the bottleneck link from the generation rate of data, we obtain much more than the amount of data queued at the bottleneck queue. The reason is that the data is also buffered at the senders' buffer.

Next we observe the evolution of the number of ongoing connections at the system, as given in Figure 4.10 and the used bandwidth at the bottleneck link, see Figure 4.11.

4.6   ADVANCED MONITORING TOOLS

In Section 4.5 we checked the termination of each TCP session periodically by comparing the current ack sequence number with the maximum sequence number of connection. This probing approach is quite costly. We mention two alternative monitoring approaches:

1. The first is to define the actions to be taken upon termination within a procedure called "done" that is automatically invoked when a connection is ended. The id of the connection that has ended as well as other properties of the connection (such as its start time) can be used by the procedure if defined as states of the connection. The approach is presented in the tcl script shortTcp2.tcl in Listing 4.4.

2. One can use a per-flow monitor. It can give statistics on each flow with information such as the amount of transferred packets, transferred bytes, losses, etc. We delay the discussion on this approach until Section 6.4.

The "state" definitions of the TCP connections in the script are done in the same way that we define the maximum window size of TCP, the slow-start initial threshold, etc. In our script we define the beginning time of the session, the session and node identity and the transfer size as such states:

```
$tcpsrc($i,$j) set starts $t
$tcpsrc($i,$j) set sess $j
$tcpsrc($i,$j) set node $i
$tcpsrc($i,$j) set size [expr [$RVSize value]]
```

The procedure "done" is defined as follows (it replaces the "Test" procedure in the previous approach of the script shortTcp.tcl in Listing 4.3):

```
Agent/TCP instproc done {} {
global tcpsrc NodeNb NumberFlows ns RV ftp Out tcp_snk RVSize
# print in $Out: node, session, start time,  end time, duration,
# trans-pkts, transm-bytes, retrans-bytes, throughput
set duration [expr [$ns now] - [$self set starts] ]
puts $Out "[$self set node] \t [$self set sess] \t [$self set starts] \t\
      [$ns now] \t $duration \t [$self set ndatapack_] \t\
      [$self set ndatabytes_] \t [$self set  nrexmitbytes_] \t\
      [expr [$self set ndatabytes_]/$duration ]"
        countFlows [$self set node] 0
}
```

Note that we use other states of TCP connections:

• ndatapack_ is the number of packets transmitted by the connection (if a packet is retransmitted several times, it is counted here only once).

• ndatabytes_ is the number of data bytes transmitted by the connection,

• nrexmitpackets_ is the number of packets retransmitted by the connection.

• nrexmitbytes_ is the number of bytes retransmitted by the connection.

Listing 4.4: Tcl script shortTcp2.tcl for short TCP connections.

```
set ns [new Simulator]

set Out [open Out.ns w]          # This file will contain the transfer times
set Conn [open Conn.tr w]        # This file will contain the number of connections
set tf [open out.tr w]           #Open the Trace file
$ns trace-all $tf


# defining the topology
set N [$ns node]
set D [$ns node]
$ns duplex-link $N $D 2Mb 1ms DropTail
$ns queue-limit $N $D 3000

set NodeNb 6                     # Number of Nodes
set NumberFlows 530              # Number of flows per source node
```

```
for {set j 1} {$j<=$NodeNb} { incr j } {          #Nodes and links
        set S($j) [$ns node]
        $ns duplex-link $S($j) $N 100Mb 1ms DropTail
        $ns queue-limit $S($j) $N 1000 }
#TCP Sources, destinations, connections
for {set i 1} {$i<=$NodeNb} { incr i } {
        for {set j 1} {$j<=$NumberFlows} { incr j } {
                set tcpsrc($i,$j) [new Agent/TCP/Newreno]
                set tcp_snk($i,$j) [new Agent/TCPSink]
                $tcpsrc($i,$j) set window_ 2000
                $ns attach-agent $S($i) $tcpsrc($i,$j)
                $ns attach-agent $D $tcp_snk($i,$j)
                $ns connect $tcpsrc($i,$j) $tcp_snk($i,$j)
                set ftp($i,$j) [$tcpsrc($i,$j) attach-source FTP]
} }
# Generators for random size of files.
set rep 1
set rng1 [new RNG]
set rng2 [new RNG]
for {set i 0} {$i < $rep} {incr i} {
$rng1 next-substream;
$rng2 next-substream;
}
# Random inter-arrival times of TCP transfer at each source i
set RV [new RandomVariable/Exponential]
$RV set avg_ 0.045
$RV use-rng $rng1

# Random size of files to transmit
set RVSize [new RandomVariable/Pareto]
$RVSize set avg_ 10000
$RVSize set shape_ 1.5
$RVSize use-rng $rng2

# We now define the beginning times of transfers and the transfer sizes
# Arrivals of sessions follow a Poisson process.
for {set i 1} {$i<=$NodeNb} { incr i } {
    set t [$ns now]
    for {set j 1} {$j<=$NumberFlows} { incr j } {
        # set the beginning time of next transfer from source and attributes
        set t [expr $t + [$RV value]]
```

```
        $tcpsrc($i,$j) set starts $t
        $tcpsrc($i,$j) set sess $j
        $tcpsrc($i,$j) set node $i
        $tcpsrc($i,$j) set size [expr [$RVSize value]]
$ns at [$tcpsrc($i,$j) set starts] "$ftp($i,$j) send [$tcpsrc($i,$j) set size]"
        # update the number of flows
        $ns at [$tcpsrc($i,$j) set starts] "countFlows $i 1"
}}
for {set j 1} {$j<=$NodeNb} { incr j } {
        set Cnts($j) 0
}
# The following procedure is called whenever a connection ends
Agent/TCP instproc done {} {
        global tcpsrc NodeNb NumberFlows ns RV ftp Out tcp_snk RVSize
        # print in $Out: node, session, start time,  end time, duration,
        # trans-pkts, transm-bytes, retrans-bytes, throughput
        set duration [expr [$ns now] - [$self set starts] ]
        puts $Out "[$self set node] \t [$self set sess] \t [$self set starts] \t\
        [$ns now] \t $duration \t [$self set ndatapack_] \t\
        [$self set ndatabytes_] \t [$self set  nrexmitbytes_] \t\
        [expr [$self set ndatabytes_]/$duration ]"
        countFlows [$self set node] 0
}
# The following recursive procedure updates the number of connections
# as a function of time. Each 0.2 sec it prints them into $Conn. This
# is done by calling the procedure with the "sign" parameter equal
# 3 (in which case the "ind" parameter does not play a role). The
# procedure is also called by the "done" procedure whenever a connection
# from source i ends by assigning the "sign" parameter 0, or when
# it begins, by assigning it 1 (i is passed through the "ind" variable).
#
proc countFlows { ind sign } {
        global Cnts Conn NodeNb
        set ns [Simulator instance]
                if { $sign==0 } { set Cnts($ind) [expr $Cnts($ind) - 1]
                } elseif { $sign==1 } { set Cnts($ind) [expr $Cnts($ind) + 1]
                } else {
                        puts -nonewline $Conn "[$ns now] \t"
                        set sum 0
                        for {set j 1} {$j<=$NodeNb} { incr j } {
                                puts -nonewline $Conn "$Cnts($j) \t"
                                set sum [expr $sum + $Cnts($j)]
```

```
                          }
                          puts $Conn "$sum"
                          $ns at [expr [$ns now] + 0.2] "countFlows 1 3"
} }
proc finish {} {                       #Define a 'finish' procedure
        global ns tf
        close $tf
        $ns flush-trace
        exit 0
}
$ns at 0.5 "countFlows 1 3"
$ns at 20 "finish"
$ns run
```

4.7   EXERCISES

4.1. Explain why the window size oscillates much more than the throughput in Figures 4.1 and 4.2.

4.2. What is the average throughput and loss rate of the TCP connection for Example ex1.tcl?

4.3. What is the average queue size for Example ex1.tcl?

4.4. Study the effect of the packet loss probability in the noisy model of rdrop.tcl on TCP throughput for loss probability ranging between 0 and 40 percent.

4.5. Modify the script rdrop.tcl in order to study the effect of the loss probability of packets (Acknowledgements) on the *reverse* link n3-n2. Plot the throughput as a function of the loss probabilities for loss rates ranging between 0 and 40 percent. Is TCP more sensitive to forward random losses of packets than to backward random losses of Acknowledgements?

4.6. Simulate two symmetric competing TCP connections sharing a common bottleneck link. Which fraction of the bandwidth does each one occupy if
(i) only one connection uses the delayed ACK option and both connections are NewReno and
(ii) both connections have the simple ACK option, the first connection uses the Tahoe version and the second the NewReno version.

4.7. In the procedure plotWindow at the end of the script ex3.tcl in Table 4.2, we passed the connection number as an argument of the procedure. What would happen if we passed it as a global variable (i.e., if we wrote "global ns j")?

4.8. Analyze the loss processes obtained in ex3.tcl (see Table 4.2). What should the queue size at link n2-n3 be so as to avoid losses?

4.9. Add to the script shortTcp.tcl (Table 4.3) random losses (i) at the forward link and (ii) at the backward link $N - D$. Vary the packet loss rate between 0% to 40%. Analyze the average time to transfer a file and the standard deviation of this time as a function of the loss rate. Explain the results! Note that in a context of many users, one may expect that if some sessions have low throughput due to losses, there will be more available throughput to other sessions, so that short TCP sessions are less sensitive than long ones to losses. Do the simulations confirm this or not? If not, explain what happens.

CHAPTER 5

Routing and network dynamics

We shall review in this chapter both unicast and multicast routing. Routing protocols that fix a permanent route (static routing) will be compared to dynamic routing. The influence of dynamic connectivity on the routing will be examined. A good reference for routing over the Internet is [35].

5.1 UNICAST ROUTING

There are several routing possibilities over the Internet. The simplest one is the static routing in which the shortest route (in terms of number of hops) is chosen throughout the connection.

NS-2 can simulate noisy links (as we saw in Section 4.3) or even links that become disconnected. To simulate a disconnection of a link between nodes $n1 and $n4 from time 1 to 4.5, for example, we should type

```
$ns rtmodel-at 1.0 down $n1 $n4
$ns rtmodel-at 4.5 up $n1 $n4
```

We now consider the network depicted in Figure 5.1 which has two alternative routes between

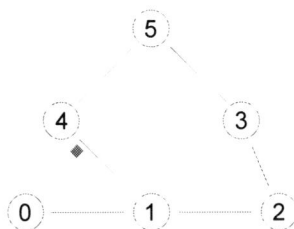

Figure 5.1: A routing example.

the source node 0 and the destination node 5. The default static routing, used by NS-2, will choose the route 0-1-4-5 for setting connections.

Listing 5.1: Tcl script for static and dynamic routing (ex2.tcl).

```
set ns [new Simulator]

#Define different colors for data flows (for NAM)
$ns color 1 Blue
```

```
$ns color 2 Red

set file1 [open out.tr w]        #Open the Trace file
$ns trace-all $file1
set file2 [open out.nam w]
$ns namtrace-all $file2

proc finish {} {                 #Define a 'finish' procedure
        global ns file1 file2
        $ns flush-trace
        close $file1
        close $file2
        exec nam out.nam &
        exit 0
}
$ns rtproto DV

#Create six nodes
set n0 [$ns node]
set n1 [$ns node]
set n2 [$ns node]
set n3 [$ns node]
set n4 [$ns node]
set n5 [$ns node]

#Create links between the nodes
$ns duplex-link $n0 $n1 0.3Mb 10ms DropTail
$ns duplex-link $n1 $n2 0.3Mb 10ms DropTail
$ns duplex-link $n2 $n3 0.3Mb 10ms DropTail
$ns duplex-link $n1 $n4 0.3Mb 10ms DropTail
$ns duplex-link $n3 $n5 0.5Mb 10ms DropTail
$ns duplex-link $n4 $n5 0.5Mb 10ms DropTail

#Give node position (for NAM)
$ns duplex-link-op  $n0 $n1 orient right
$ns duplex-link-op  $n1 $n2 orient right
$ns duplex-link-op $n2 $n3 orient up
$ns duplex-link-op $n1 $n4 orient up-left
$ns duplex-link-op  $n3 $n5 orient left-up
$ns duplex-link-op  $n4 $n5 orient right-up

#Setup a TCP connection
```

```
set tcp [new Agent/TCP/Newreno]
$ns attach-agent $n0 $tcp
set sink [new Agent/TCPSink/DelAck]
$ns attach-agent $n5 $sink
$ns connect $tcp $sink
$tcp set fid_ 1

#Setup a FTP over TCP connection
set ftp [new Application/FTP]
$ftp attach-agent $tcp
$ftp set type_ FTP

$ns rtmodel-at 1.0 down $n1 $n4
$ns rtmodel-at 4.5 up $n1 $n4

$ns at 0.1 "$ftp start"
$ns at 12.0 "finish"
$ns run
```

In contrast to the static routing, the Internet can find an alternative route once it discovers that the route actually followed is disconnected.

We can use session routing that will recompute the routes once the network discovers that there was a change in the topology. This type of routing uses exactly the same algorithm as the static one, but prevents simulation of the problems of complete disconnection on the static routing if the network is always connected. To use session routing we have to type: $ns rtproto Session.

Note that if one does not specify which routing protocol will be used with the last command by default NS-2 will use static routing.

Another option for doing dynamic routing is by using the Distance Vector routing which uses the Distributed Bellman-Ford algorithm to compute the routes.

In NS-2 we do that by adding the command (see Listing 5.1) $ns rtproto DV.

In the Example ex2.tcl given in Listing 5.1, the link 1-4 is down during the time interval [1, 4.5]. In NAM, we can see this link becoming red during this time. A TCP connection is set between node 0 and 5. When running the script, with the static routing (commenting out the command $ns rtproto DV) we see that even though the connection is resumed at time 4.5, the TCP connection resumes only at time 8 approximately. The reason is that timeouts had occurred in the absence of ACKs returning to node 0, and their duration doubles with each new timeout.

In the nam trace we can see in the dynamic routing case, the signaling packets that are used to determine the path, not only at the beginning, but also at connectivity changes.

5.2   NETWORK DYNAMICS

We saw in the last section that we can determine link states explicitly: the link can go down and up at preselected times. There are, however, other possibilities to change dynamically the connectivity: according to an Exponential On-Off process, or a deterministic On-Off process, or according to some given trace file.

The syntax for this is: `$ns rtmodel model model-params args` where model can be: Deterministic, Exponential, Manual or Trace.

The deterministic model has four parameters: start time (0.5sec from the beginning of the simulation by default), up interval (10sec by default), down interval (1sec by default) and finish time (end of the simulation by default).

In the exponential case, the up and down parameters correspond to the expected durations.

The arguments (args) are the nodes that specify the link which will fail or a node that will go down and up. For example, the syntax for the deterministic model applied to link n1-n2 is `$ns rtmodel Deterministic {0.8 1.0 1.0} $n1 $n2` (the finish time is the default).

In a command of the form `$ns rtmodel Deterministic {0.8 1.0} $n1 $n2`, the start and end times are the defaults, and in a command of the form `$ns rtmodel Deterministic {- 1.0} $n1 $n2`, the only non-default parameter is the down interval. The exponential connectivity is obtained above by replacing "Deterministic" by "Exponential".

The command that corresponds to connectivity based on a trace file is `$ns rtmodel Trace <config_file> $n0 $n1`. Finally, one can also generate a sequence of routing states in NS-2, and use it as an input (see [24]).

Node failures   There is a possibility of a node going down and up. This is done exactly as we saw for the case of links, except that only one node appears as argument at the end.

5.3   MULTICAST PROTOCOLS

In multicast, there may be several multicast groups of members; the groups may overlap. In IP multicast, the receiver must request membership in multicast group whereas a sender can send without first joining a group. Senders do not receive feedback from the network about the receivers in IP multicast routing. Not all network nodes may be able to handle multicast; in NS-2 one can declare which nodes indeed have multicast capabilities.

A routing protocol defines the mechanism by which the multicast tree is computed in the simulation. There are two main classes of routing:

1. A "dense mode" type which is appropriate for the case of a large number of multicast users; in that case multicast trees are constructed for any pair of source and its multicast group. The construction of the trees requires broadcasting to all nodes in the network.

2. A "sparse mode" in which there is a small number of nodes. Therefore the routing can be handled using a single shared tree.

Four multicast routing protocols are available in NS-2: the Dense Mode (DM), the Centralised (CtrMcast), the Shared Tree mode (ST) and the Bi-directional Shared Tree mode (BST). Unfortunately, the way NS-2 simulates the protocols does not include much of the signaling, especially in the initialization. The DM protocol is the only one that has a dynamic version in NS-2, called dynamicDM.

5.3.1 THE DENSE MODE

The DM protocol has two modes which are quite similar: the protocol pimDM (Protocol Independent Multicast - Dense Mode) and the `dvmrp` (Distance Vector Multicast Routing Protocol) mode [57], pimDM being somewhat simpler. They are based on an initial flooding of the network (using the RFP approach) and then on the computation of the shortest reverse path. We suppose that point-to-point routing tables are available. This is done as follows.

- If a router receives a multipoint packet from a source S to a group G, it checks first (using point-to-point routing tables) that the input reception interface corresponds to packet from S: this means that this router is in the shortest path from the source (this is thus called a "shortest reverse path" approach). If the result is negative then it sends a message "delete(S,G)", i.e., a message to the source requesting to stop sending to it packets from S to G.

- If the result is positive then the router sends a copy of the message to the set T of all the interfaces through which it has not yet received a request "delete(S,G)". If T is empty, then it destroys the packet and sends a message "delete(S,G)" to the interface through which it received the message.

5.3.2 ROUTING BASED ON A RV POINT

The centralized mcast (CrtMcast) is similar to the so called PIM-SM (the Sparse Mode of PIM [22]). There is a RendezVous Point (RVP). A shared tree is built for a multicast group rooted at this RVP. A centralized computation agent is used to compute the forwarding trees and set up multicast forwarding state, S, G (the state S corresponds to the source of a packet and G to the address of the multicast group to which it is destined) at the relevant nodes as new receivers join a group. Data packets from the senders to a group are unicast to the RVP. The multicasting from the RVP to the group is done according to a shortest path tree.

The ST mode is a simplified version of the above sparse mode routing protocol. This protocol has a bidirectional version in ns called BST, which is used in the standard version CBT [13] and in the BGMP protocol for inter-domain multicast [56].

In protocols based on a RV point, all multicast traffic traverses the RV point, which is thus a bottleneck. A failure in that node is critical for the whole group. Another problem with this approach is that traffic travels on non-optimal paths. The advantages of this approach are (1) the simplicity in the state information: only one entry per-source per-group, and (2) signalling does not involve the whole network.

Note that in PIM-SM, there is a possibility of switching to optimized source-based trees (S,G) instead of routing through the RV point. This occurs if the source data rate exceeds some threshold. Thus the RV point can cease to be a bottleneck if traffic rate is large. ST mode does not simulate this feature.

5.4   SIMULATING MULTICAST ROUTING

Multicast requires enhancements of the nodes and links of the network. NS-2 has therefore specific requirements from the Simulator class before creating the topology. We thus begin by the special command

```
set ns [new Simulator]
$ns multicast
```

In the tcl script we define group addresses using the command `set group1 [Node allocaddr]`. We then define an application and a transport protocol agent attached on one hand to a given source node and on the other hand to a group destination.

We consider below the DM protocol. When a source S sending to a group G becomes active, it begins flooding the network along the attached tree corresponding to group G. When a leaf that has not joined the multicast group receives a packet to that group, it sends a message to the incoming interface to delete it from the tree (S,G) (a "prune" packet). This then propagates backwards to the source: a node that receives a message from all its output links within the tree of (S,G) requesting to delete these links, then sends back to its incoming interface a message to delete it from the tree (S,G).

A source will stop sending packets if there are no connected receivers in that group; it will resume sending packet when a receiver connects.

We now consider the network depicted in Figure 5.1.

In the Listing 5.2 we can see a few new commands, we will explain each one of them:

- `set group [Node allocaddr]` this command will assign a new multicast address to the variable group. The address comes from the simulator, which maintains control of all the multicast addresses, but the method is coded on the Node class, because we have to instantiate the method from the class Node.

- `set mproto DM` assigns to the variable mproto the value DM, which stands for Dense Mode, explained in Subsection 5.4.1.

- `set mrthandle [$ns mrtproto $mproto]` returns a handle to the multicast protocol object. It specifies dense mode multicast for all nodes.

- `$udp1 set dst_addr_ $group` gives as destination address of the flow the multicast address obtained above.

- The `join-group` and `leave-group` commands associate or disassociate a given node to a multicast address.

Listing 5.2: Example for multicast with DM model: pimdm.tcl.

```
set ns [new Simulator]
$ns multicast

set f [open out.tr w]
$ns trace-all $f
$ns namtrace-all [open out.nam w]

$ns color 1 red
$ns color 30 purple      # the nam colors for the prune packets
$ns color 31 green       # the nam colors for the graft packets

set group [Node allocaddr]      # allocate a multicast address;
set nod 6                       # nod is the number of nodes

# create multicast capable nodes;
for {set i 1} {$i <= $nod} {incr i} {
    set n($i) [$ns node]
}
#Create links between the nodes
$ns duplex-link $n(1) $n(2) 0.3Mb 10ms DropTail
$ns duplex-link $n(2) $n(3) 0.3Mb 10ms DropTail
$ns duplex-link $n(2) $n(4) 0.5Mb 10ms DropTail
$ns duplex-link $n(2) $n(5) 0.3Mb 10ms DropTail
$ns duplex-link $n(3) $n(4) 0.3Mb 10ms DropTail
$ns duplex-link $n(4) $n(5) 0.5Mb 10ms DropTail
$ns duplex-link $n(4) $n(6) 0.5Mb 10ms DropTail
$ns duplex-link $n(5) $n(6) 0.5Mb 10ms DropTail

set mproto DM                   # configure multicast protocol;

# all nodes will contain multicast protocol agents;
set mrthandle [$ns mrtproto $mproto]

set udp1 [new Agent/UDP]
set udp2 [new Agent/UDP]
$ns attach-agent $n(1) $udp1
$ns attach-agent $n(2) $udp2
```

```
set src1 [new Application/Traffic/CBR]
$src1 attach-agent $udp1
$udp1 set dst_addr_ $group
$udp1 set dst_port_ 0
$src1 set random_ false

set src2 [new Application/Traffic/CBR]
$src2 attach-agent $udp2
$udp2 set dst_addr_ $group
$udp2 set dst_port_ 1
$src2 set random_ false

set rcvr [new Agent/LossMonitor]        # create receiver agents

# joining and leaving the group;
$ns at 0.6 "$n(3) join-group $rcvr $group"
$ns at 1.3 "$n(4) join-group $rcvr $group"
$ns at 1.6 "$n(5) join-group $rcvr $group"
$ns at 1.9 "$n(4) leave-group $rcvr $group"
$ns at 2.3 "$n(6) join-group $rcvr $group"
$ns at 3.5 "$n(3) leave-group $rcvr $group"

$ns at 0.4 "$src1 start"
$ns at 2.0 "$src2 start"
$ns at 4.0 "finish"
proc finish {} {
        global ns
        $ns flush-trace
        exec nam out.nam &
        exit 0
}
$ns run
```

An example of a multicast configuration with a six node network is depicted in Figure 5.2.

The Loss Monitor Agent   We used here the LossMonitor Agent, which is a packet sink agent that maintains statistics about the received traffic, such as the amount of packets received as well as lost information. In particular, we can access the following state variables: nlost_ (number of lost packets), npkts_ (number of received packets), bytes_ (number of received bytes), lastPktTime_ (time at which the last packet was received) and expected_ (the expected sequence number of the

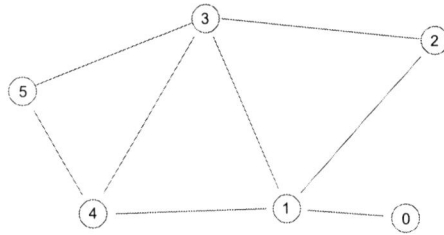

Figure 5.2: A multicast routing example.

next packet). One can use instead of the LossMonitor agent, the Null agent, as we did before, i.e., type `set rcvr [new Agent/Null]` instead of `set rcvr [new Agent/LossMonitor]`.

5.4.1   DM MODE

The command `set mproto DM` indicates that we use the Dense Mode protocol. By default, the pimDM is used. In order to use the dvmrp mode, one adds the line

```
DM set CacheMissMode dvmrp
```

just before the line `set mproto DM`.

In the DM mode, flooding occurs periodically so as to detect the nodes that are connected to the group. The timer value for the period is given in a variable called **PruneTimeout**. It's default value is 0.5sec; if another value is required, say 0.8 sec, then one adds to the tcl script the command

```
DM set PruneTimeout 0.8
```

just before the line `set mproto DM`.

5.4.2   ROUTING WITH A CENTRALIZED RV POINT

For the centralized mode one needs:

```
# configure multicast protocol;
set mproto CtrMcast
# all nodes will contain multicast protocol agents;
set mrthandle [$ns mrtproto $mproto]
# set RV and bootstrap points
$mrthandle set_c_rp $n(2)
```

Here we chose $n(2)$ to be the RV point.

In both the centralized as well as in the ST mode, the signalling (prune packets) are not simulated.

We present in Listing 5.3 the same example as in pimdm.tcl (Listing 5.2) but with the BST routing protocol.

Listing 5.3: Example for multicast with RV point: bst.tcl.

```tcl
set ns [new Simulator -multicast on]

set f [open out.tr w]
$ns trace-all $f
$ns namtrace-all [open out.nam w]
$ns color 1 red
$ns color 30 purple     # the nam colors for the prune packets
$ns color 31 green      # the nam colors for the graft packets

set group [Node allocaddr]    # allocate a multicast address;
set nod 6                     # nod is the number of nodes

# create multicast capable nodes;
for {set i 1} {$i <= $nod} {incr i} {
    set n($i) [$ns node]
}
#Create links between the nodes
$ns duplex-link $n(1) $n(2) 0.3Mb 10ms DropTail
$ns duplex-link $n(2) $n(3) 0.3Mb 10ms DropTail
$ns duplex-link $n(2) $n(4) 0.5Mb 10ms DropTail
$ns duplex-link $n(2) $n(5) 0.3Mb 10ms DropTail
$ns duplex-link $n(3) $n(4) 0.3Mb 10ms DropTail
$ns duplex-link $n(4) $n(5) 0.5Mb 10ms DropTail
$ns duplex-link $n(4) $n(6) 0.5Mb 10ms DropTail
$ns duplex-link $n(5) $n(6) 0.5Mb 10ms DropTail

# configure multicast protocol;
BST set RP_($group) $n(2)
$ns mrtproto BST

set udp1 [new Agent/UDP]
set udp2 [new Agent/UDP]
$ns attach-agent $n(1) $udp1
$ns attach-agent $n(2) $udp2

set src1 [new Application/Traffic/CBR]
$src1 attach-agent $udp1
$udp1 set dst_addr_ $group
$udp1 set dst_port_ 0
$src1 set random_ false
```

```
set src2 [new Application/Traffic/CBR]
$src2 attach-agent $udp2
$udp2 set dst_addr_ $group
$udp2 set dst_port_ 1
$src2 set random_ false

set rcvr [new Agent/LossMonitor]       # create receiver agents

# joining and leaving the group;
$ns at 0.6 "$n(3) join-group $rcvr $group"
$ns at 1.3 "$n(4) join-group $rcvr $group"
$ns at 1.6 "$n(5) join-group $rcvr $group"
$ns at 1.9 "$n(4) leave-group $rcvr $group"
$ns at 2.3 "$n(6) join-group $rcvr $group"
$ns at 3.5 "$n(3) leave-group $rcvr $group"

$ns at 0.4 "$src1 start"
$ns at 2.0 "$src2 start"

$ns at 4.0 "finish"
proc finish {} {
        global ns
        $ns flush-trace
        exec nam out.nam &
        exit 0
}
$ns run
```

5.5   OBSERVATIONS ON THE SIMULATION OF PIMDM.TCL

Dense mode: pimdm and dvmrp   If we run the simulation and observe the trace, we shall see that in addition to the CBR packets, there are two other types of packets: the "prune" packet, and the "graft" packet. The role of the prune packet sent by a node N is to signal to the node that had sent a previous packet to N to stop sending packets to N. The "graft" packet is a signal originating from a node that wishes to join the group (after it had been disconnected). In the NAM display of our simulation, the graft packets are light green, and the prune are purple.

We can see that at time 0.4, node 0 starts sending CBR packets that flood the network. But there are no receivers at the multicast group, so eventually, prune packets return to the source and transmission is stopped (time 0.579). At time 0.6, a graft packet is sent from node 2 (which wishes to join the group) to node 1, and then from node 1 to node 0. Node 0 then restarts transmission. At time 0.9978, there is again an attempt to check whether there are connected receiver nodes in the group other than 2 and the network is again flooded; prune packets return to stop the transmission to nodes 3, 4, 5.

The centralized mode We see in the trace encapsulated packets that are sent from a source to the RV point of size 230 bytes. The header is then removed by the RV point which then forwards the packet (size 210 bytes) to the members of the group.

5.6 EXERCISES

5.1. Run the program ex2.tcl (see Table 5.1) commenting out the command "$ns rtproto DV" and explain what happens.

5.2. Run the program ex2.tcl (see Table 5.1) with the command "$ns rtproto DV" and explain the differences from the previous static routing.

5.3. Change and run simulation ex2.tcl (see Table 5.1) for a duration of 200 sec with static routing but with a dynamic exponential ON-OFF connectivity, with ON average time of 3 sec and OFF average time of 0.5 sec. Analyze the behavior of the TCP connection and the time-out behavior.

5.4. Run the pimdm.tcl script (see Table 5.2). How many CBR packets have been transmitted from each source, and how many have been lost? How many CBR packets have been received at nodes that did not need them (more precisely, how many prune packets have been generated)?

5.5. Consider the trace obtained from the pimdm.tcl script. At time 1.8375 we start to have losses at node 0. At time 2.481, packets start getting lost also at node 1. Explain these losses!

5.6. Run the program pimdm.tcl with the dvmrp mode of DM. What are the differences that you observe between dvmrp and the pimDM version?

5.7. Run the centralised version of the multicast. Explain what happens when the RP is changed to node n(5) (in the NAM it will correspond to node 4 since NAM counts from 0). Explain why this is less efficient than choosing the RP node to be n(2). How can we measure efficiency?

CHAPTER 6

RED: Random Early Discard

6.1 DESCRIPTION OF RED

The RED buffer management scheme was introduced in 1993 by Floyd and Jacobson [28], and is further described in the RFC 2309 [15]. Many important references to RED can be found at http://www.icir.org/floyd/red.html. The basic idea is that one should not wait till the buffer is full in order to detect congestion (drop packets), but start detecting congestion before the buffer overflows. Congestion signals could still be through packet dropping, but could now also be through marking of packets without the need to actually drop them.

Some of the goals of the RED buffer management are:

1. Accommodate short bursts that might be delay sensitive, but not to allow the average queue size to increase too much. Using some low pass filtering of the queue size, the aim is to detect congestion that lasts long enough.

2. Drop tail and random drop gateways that have a bias against bursty traffic. Indeed in such buffers, the more the traffic of a connection is bursty, the more likely it is that the queue will overflow during the arrival time of packets of that connection.

3. Avoid synchronization: in drop tail buffer, many connections may receive a congestion signal at the same time leading to undesirable oscillations in the throughputs. Such oscillation may cause lower average throughputs and high jitter. To avoid synchronization, congestions signals are chosen using randomization.

4. Control the average queue size. Note that this also means controlling the average queueing delay.

To achieve these objectives, RED monitors the average queue size avg, and checks whether it lies between some minimum threshold min_{th} and a maximum threshold max_{th}. If it does, then an arriving packet is dropped or marked with probability $p = p(avg)$, which is an increasing function of the average queue size. All arriving packets that arrive when avg exceeds max_{th} are marked/dropped.

The probability $p(avg)$ is chosen as follows. As the average queue size varies between min_{th} and max_{th}, a probability p_b varies linearly between 0 and some value max_p, i.e.,

$$p_b(avg) = max_p \frac{avg - min_{th}}{max_{th} - min_{th}}.$$

This probability is used as $p(avg)$ if at the arrival of the previous packet, $avg \geq min_{th}$. Otherwise, $p(avg)$ is set to the value $p(avg)/(1 + p(avg))$.

The average queue size is monitored as follows. The avg parameter is initially set to zero. Then with each arriving packet, the new value avg is assigned the value

$$(1 - w_q)avg + w_q q$$

where q is the actual queue size and w_q is some small constant. If the queue becomes empty some other formula is used to update its size, which takes into account the time since it became empty and an estimate on the number of packets that could have been sent during this idle time, see [28]. For estimating the latter, we shall need in ns to give as parameter a rough estimate of the mean packet size.

Examples of RED parameters studied in [28] are $w_q = 0.002$, $min_{th} = 5$packets, $max_{th} = 15$packets, $max_p = 1/50$ and the queue size is 100. More generally they also investigate min_{th} ranging between 3 to 50, and keep $max_{th} = 3min_{th}$.

The implementation of red in ns can be found in ns-allinone-2.XXX/ns-2.XXX/queue/red.cc (XXX stands for the version, e.g., 1b9a).

6.2   SETTING RED PARAMETERS IN NS-2

The parameters of RED in NS-2 are provided in the following objects:

1. bytes_: takes either the value "true" if we work in the "byte mode" or "false" in the packet mode (the default value). In the "byte mode", the size of an arriving packet affects the likelihood of marking it.

2. queue-in-bytes_: the average queue size will be measured in bytes if this is set to "true". In that case, also thresh_ and maxthres_ are scaled by the estimated average packet size parameter mean_pktsize_. It is "false" by default.

3. thres_: is the minimum queue size threshold min_{th}.

4. maxthres_: is the maximum queue size threshold max_{th}.

5. mean_pktsize_: is the estimate of the average packet size in bytes. The default value is 500.

6. q_weight_: the weight factor w_q in computing the averaged queue length.

7. wait_: this is a parameter that allows to maintain an interval between dropped packets when set to "true" (the default value).

8. linterm_: this is the reciprocal of max_p. Its default value is 10.

9. `setbit_`: is "false" in the case that RED is used to actually drop packets, and is "true" if RED marks the packet with a congestion bit instead. (The ECN version of TCP reacts to these congestion bits).

10. `drop-tail_`: this is a parameter that allows, when setting its value to "true" (the default value), to use the drop-tail policy when queue overflows or when the average queue size exceeds max_{th}.

The default values of `q_weight_`, `maxthresh_` and `thres_` have been 0.002, 15 and 5, respectively, till the end of 2001. In the more recent releases they are configured automatically.

RED has other parameters and variants that are implemented in NS-2. In particular, S. Floyd recommends in http://www.icir.org/floyd/red/gentle.html for the best behavior of RED (in simulations and in implementations), to use the `gentle_` parameter set to "true" (this is the default since April, 2001). In the `gentle_` modification to RED in NS-2, the packet-dropping probability varies from max_p to 1 as the average queue size varies from `maxthresh_` to twice `maxthresh_`. This option makes RED much more robust to the setting of the parameters `maxthresh` and `max_p`.

Another version is the adaptive RED that adapts the choice of parameters to the network traffic, as described in [51].

In order to monitor a given red buffer, say one between nodes $n2 and $n3, one can type

```
set redq [[$ns link $n2 $n3] queue]
set traceq [open red-queue.tr w]
$redq trace curq_
$redq trace ave_
$redq attach $traceq
```

Here `curq_` is the current queue value and `ave_` is the averaged value. This gives an output file (in our case "red-queue.tr") with three columns. The first indicates whether it is a value of the current queue size (by using the flag "Q") or the averaged queue size (using the flag "a"). Then comes the current time and finally the monitored value.

6.3 SIMULATION EXAMPLES

We consider the following network, depicted in Figure 6.1: We shall compare the behavior of several queue management schemes.

6.3.1 DROP TAIL BUFFER

The first buffer management scheme is a simple drop tail mechanism. We consider three input links with delay 1msec each and bandwidth of 10Mbps each. The common bottleneck link has 20msec of delay and bandwidth of 700 kbps. We consider three FTP connections using TCP and set the maximum window sizes to 8000. The bottleneck queue size is 100. The three connections start at random times, uniformly distributed between 0 and 7 sec. They delay till the bottleneck is 1msec. We chose a TCP packet size of 552 bytes. Note: in version 2.1b9a of ns, when we type the command

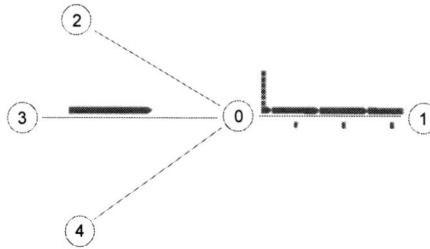

Figure 6.1: Network setting for the study of RED.

```
$tcp_src($j) set packetSize_ 552
```

then the actual packet size created in the simulation is 592, since an extra 40 bytes of header are added. The whole simulation lasts 50 sec.

Using the monitor-queue option that we saw already in Section 4.3, we create a file called queue.tr whose first column is the time and the fifth column is the queue size in packets. We shall also use a procedure, called plotWindow, to monitor the window sizes: it creates a file where the first column is time, and the other three columns correspond to the window sizes of the three connections.

Listing 6.1: Tcl script droptail.tcl.

```
set ns [new Simulator]

set nf [open out.nam w]
$ns namtrace-all $nf

set tf [open out.tr w]
set windowVsTime [open win w]
set param [open parameters w]
$ns trace-all $tf

#Define a 'finish' procedure
proc finish {} {
        global ns nf tf
        $ns flush-trace
        close $nf
        close $tf
        exec nam out.nam &
        exit 0
}
#Create bottleneck and dest nodes
set n2 [$ns node]
```

```
set n3 [$ns node]

#Create links between these nodes
$ns duplex-link $n2 $n3 0.7Mb 20ms DropTail

set NumbSrc 3
set Duration 50
set rep 2

#Source nodes
for {set j 1} {$j<=$NumbSrc} { incr j } {
    set S($j) [$ns node]
}
set rng [new RNG]

# Create a random generator for starting the ftp
for { set i 0 } {$i<$rep } {incr i } {
    $rng next-substream;
}
# parameters for random variables for beginning of ftp connections
set RVstart [new RandomVariable/Uniform]
$RVstart set min_  0
$RVstart set max_  7
$RVstart use-rng $rng

#We define random starting times for each connection
for {set i 1} {$i<=$NumbSrc} { incr i } {
    set startT($i)  [expr [$RVstart value]]
    set dly($i) 1
    puts $param "startT($i)  $startT($i) sec"
}
#Links between source and bottleneck
for {set j 1} {$j<=$NumbSrc} { incr j } {
    $ns duplex-link $S($j) $n2 10Mb $dly($j)ms DropTail
    $ns queue-limit $S($j) $n2 20
}
#Set Queue Size of link (n2-n3) to 100
$ns queue-limit $n2 $n3 100

#TCP Sources
for {set j 1} {$j<=$NumbSrc} { incr j } {
    set tcp_src($j) [new Agent/TCP/Reno]
```

```
    $tcp_src($j) set window_ 8000
}
#TCP Destinations
for {set j 1} {$j<=$NumbSrc} { incr j } {
    set tcp_snk($j) [new Agent/TCPSink]
}
#Connections
for {set j 1} {$j<=$NumbSrc} { incr j } {
    $ns attach-agent $S($j) $tcp_src($j)
    $ns attach-agent $n3 $tcp_snk($j)
    $ns connect $tcp_src($j) $tcp_snk($j)
}
#FTP sources
for {set j 1} {$j<=$NumbSrc} { incr j } {
    set ftp($j) [$tcp_src($j) attach-source FTP]
}
#Parametrisation of TCP sources
for {set j 1} {$j<=$NumbSrc} { incr j } {
    $tcp_src($j) set packetSize_ 552
}
#Schedule events for the FTP agents:
for {set i 1} {$i<=$NumbSrc} { incr i } {
    $ns at $startT($i) "$ftp($i) start"
    $ns at $Duration "$ftp($i) stop"
}
proc plotWindow {tcpSource file k} {
global ns NumbSrc
set time 0.03
set now [$ns now]
set cwnd [$tcpSource set cwnd_]
if {$k == 1} {
    puts -nonewline $file "$now \t $cwnd \t"
  } else {
    if {$k < $NumbSrc } {
    puts -nonewline $file "$cwnd \t" }
}
if { $k == $NumbSrc } {
    puts -nonewline $file "$cwnd \n" }
$ns at [expr $now+$time] "plotWindow $tcpSource $file $k"
}
# The procedure will now be called for all tcp sources
for {set j 1} {$j<=$NumbSrc} { incr j } {
```

```
    $ns at 0.1 "plotWindow $tcp_src($j) $windowVsTime $j"
}
set qfile [$ns monitor-queue $n2 $n3  [open queue.tr w] 0.05]
[$ns link $n2 $n3] queue-sample-timeout;


$ns at [expr $Duration] "finish"
$ns run
```

During the 50 sec of simulation time, the source received 6924 TCP packets. Next we plot the queue size (Figure 6.2) and the window size (Figure 6.3).

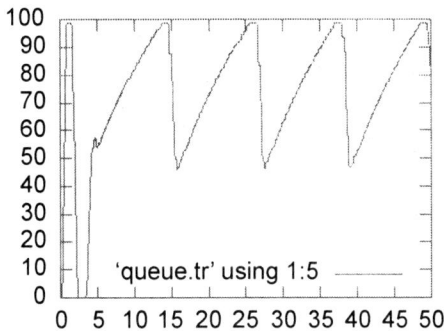

Figure 6.2: Queue size evolution.

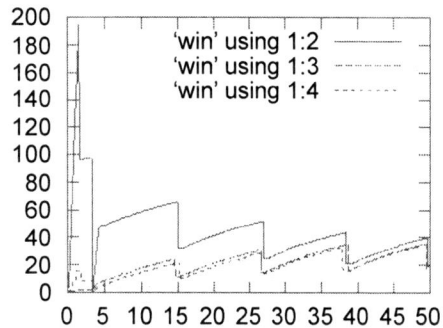

Figure 6.3: Window size of all TCP connections.

We see from the figures that there is a high level of synchronization between the window sizes: they all lose packets at the same time. Moreover, we have large oscillations of the queue sizes that correspond to those of the windows, and the average queue size is around 75 packets. This means that there is an additional average queueing delay which equals

$$D_q = \frac{75 \times 592 \times 8}{700 \times 10^3} = 507.42 msec$$

Remark 6.1 The drop-tail queue can be simulated using a RED buffer with $min_{th} = max_{th}$ set to the maximum queue size and max_p set to a value close to zero. This allows us to use the monitoring tools for the instantaneous and average queue length of RED. Of course, the drop-tail_ parameter has the value "true".

6.3.2   RED BUFFER WITH AUTOMATIC PARAMETER CONFIGURATION

We run a second simulation with the same parameters. Note that we choose for the random delay a seed 2 (with the variable rep) in all the simulations since unlike the seed 0, it will guarantee that the same random sequence is used in all simulations.

During the 50 sec of simulation time, the source received 6786 TCP packets, slightly less than with the drop tail case (where we had 6786 packets). Next we plot the queue size (Figure 6.4 and 6.5) and the window size (Figure 6.6).

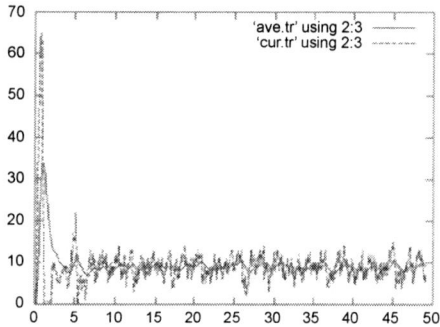

Figure 6.4: Current and Average queue size evolution.

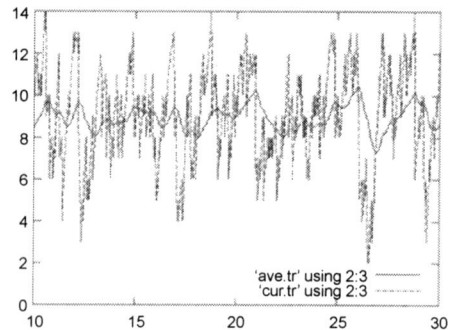

Figure 6.5: Current and Average queue size evolution: a zoom.

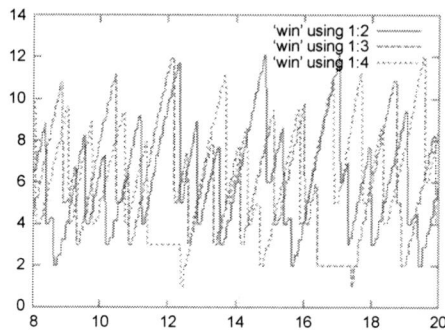

Figure 6.6: Window size of all TCP connections for Red buffer with automatic parameter configuration.

We see from the figures that there is no synchronization between the window sizes, and that the average queue size is much lower than in the drop tail case: it is around 10 (instead of 75 in the drop tail case). Thus the average delay of the connections is also smaller,

$$D_q = \frac{10 \times 592 \times 8}{700 \times 10^3} = 67.66 msec.$$

We observe that instead of the large oscillations of the queue size and the window sizes, we now get much faster and smaller variations in both window size as well as queue size. We finally notice that during the simulation, the queue never overflowed, unlike the case of drop tail. Yet RED did allow the queue to grow very much during the transient spike at the beginning of the connection, which shows that short bursts are indeed not penalized with RED.

We provide in Listing 6.2 the tcl script we used.

Listing 6.2: Tcl script red.tcl.

```
set ns [new Simulator]
set nf [open out.nam w]
$ns namtrace-all $nf
set tf [open out.tr w]
set windowVsTime [open win w]
set param [open parameters w]
$ns trace-all $tf


#Define a 'finish' procedure
proc finish {} {
        global ns nf tf
        $ns flush-trace
        close $nf
        close $tf
        exec nam out.nam &
        exec grep  "a" red-queue.tr > ave.tr
        exec grep  "Q" red-queue.tr > cur.tr
        exit 0
}
#Create bottleneck and dest nodes
set n2 [$ns node]
set n3 [$ns node]


#Create links between these nodes
$ns duplex-link $n2 $n3 0.7Mb 20ms RED


set NumbSrc 3
set Duration 50
set rep 2


#Source nodes
for {set j 1} {$j<=$NumbSrc} { incr j } {
   set S($j) [$ns node]
```

```
}
# Create a random generator for starting the ftp and for bottleneck link delays
set rng [new RNG]
for { set i 0 } {$i<$rep } {incr i } {
    $rng next-substream;
}
# parameters for random variables for begenning of ftp connections
set RVstart [new RandomVariable/Uniform]
$RVstart set min_ 0
$RVstart set max_ 7
$RVstart use-rng $rng

#We define random starting times for each connection
for {set i 1} {$i<=$NumbSrc} { incr i } {
    set startT($i)  [expr [$RVstart value]]
    set dly($i) 1
    puts $param "startT($i)  $startT($i) sec"
}
#Links between source and bottleneck
for {set j 1} {$j<=$NumbSrc} { incr j } {
    $ns duplex-link $S($j) $n2 10Mb $dly($j)ms DropTail
    $ns queue-limit $S($j) $n2 20
}
#Set Queue Size of link (n2-n3) to 100
$ns queue-limit $n2 $n3 100

set redq [[$ns link $n2 $n3] queue]
set traceq [open red-queue.tr w]
$redq trace curq_
$redq trace ave_
$redq attach $traceq

#TCP Sources
for {set j 1} {$j<=$NumbSrc} { incr j } {
    set tcp_src($j) [new Agent/TCP/Reno]
    $tcp_src($j) set window_ 8000
}
#TCP Destinations
for {set j 1} {$j<=$NumbSrc} { incr j } {
    set tcp_snk($j) [new Agent/TCPSink]
}
#Connections
```

```
for {set j 1} {$j<=$NumbSrc} { incr j } {
    $ns attach-agent $S($j) $tcp_src($j)
    $ns attach-agent $n3 $tcp_snk($j)
    $ns connect $tcp_src($j) $tcp_snk($j)
}
#FTP sources
for {set j 1} {$j<=$NumbSrc} { incr j } {
    set ftp($j) [$tcp_src($j) attach-source FTP]
}
#Parametrisation of TCP sources
for {set j 1} {$j<=$NumbSrc} { incr j } {
    $tcp_src($j) set packetSize_ 552
}
#Schedule events for the FTP agents:
for {set i 1} {$i<=$NumbSrc} { incr i } {
    $ns at $startT($i) "$ftp($i) start"
    $ns at $Duration "$ftp($i) stop"
}
proc plotWindow {tcpSource file k} {
global ns NumbSrc
set time 0.03
set now [$ns now]
set cwnd [$tcpSource set cwnd_]
if {$k == 1} {
    puts -nonewline $file "$now \t $cwnd \t"
  } else {
    if {$k < $NumbSrc } {
    puts -nonewline $file "$cwnd \t" }
}
if { $k == $NumbSrc } {
    puts -nonewline $file "$cwnd \n" }
$ns at [expr $now+$time] "plotWindow $tcpSource $file $k"
}
# The procedure will now be called for all tcp sources
for {set j 1} {$j<=$NumbSrc} { incr j } {
    $ns at 0.1 "plotWindow $tcp_src($j) $windowVsTime $j"
}
$ns at [expr $Duration] "finish"
$ns run
```

6.3.3   RED BUFFER WITH OTHER PARAMETERS

Suppose we wish to define our own parameters for RED rather than use the default ones. For example, assume we wish to have in our previous example max_{th}=60, min_{th}=40 and $q\_weight\_$=0.02. Then we should add the commands

```
Queue/RED set thresh_ 60
Queue/RED set maxthresh_ 80
Queue/RED set q_weight_ 0.002
```

Important note: these commands should be put at the beginning, before the links are defined!

The resulting window and queue size processes are given in Figures 6.8 and 6.7, respectively.

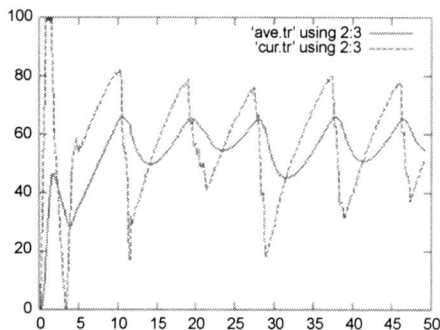

Figure 6.7: Current and Average queue size evolution.

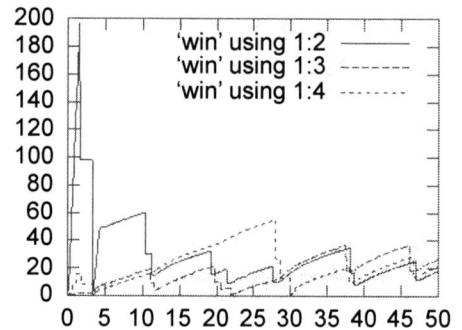

Figure 6.8: Window size of all TCP connections for Red buffer.

Note that with the parameters that we chose, the queue lengths are kept around an average of 50. The number of TCP packets received during the simulation was 6769.

6.4   MONITORING FLOWS

We introduce in this section the flow monitor, which is an efficient way to monitor per-flow quantities such as losses and amount of transmitted traffic. We shall modify the ns script of shortTcp2.tcl (Table 4.4) to include a RED buffer with monitoring.

A flow monitors a simplex link, so we first define the link we wish to monitor:

```
set flink [$ns simplex-link $N $D 2Mb 1ms RED]
```

and then the flow-monitor is defined as follows with respect to this link:

```
set monfile [open mon.tr w]
set fmon [$ns makeflowmon Fid]
$ns attach-fmon $flink $fmon
$fmon attach $monfile
```

When we activate the monitoring, we get the statistics up to the activation time in a file. This is done as follows:

`$ns at $time "$fmon dump"`

We next present in Listing 6.3 the full script shortRed.tcl that allows us to study short TCP sessions interacting with a RED buffer.

Listing 6.3: Tcl script shortRed.tcl.

```
set ns [new Simulator]

set Out [open Out.ns w];    #file containing transfer times of different connections
set Conn [open Conn.tr w]; #file containing the number of connections
set tf [open out.tr w];     #Open the Trace file
$ns trace-all $tf

set NodeNb      6;   # Number od source nodes
set NumberFlows 253; # Number of flows per source node
set sduration    50;  # Duration of simulation
set rep 2; # Simulation replica

# When the following parameters are commented, the RED is
# configured automatically.
# Queue/RED set thresh_ 5
# Queue/RED set maxthresh_ 15
# Queue/RED set q_weight_ 0.002

# defining the topology
set N [$ns node]
set D [$ns node]
set flink [$ns simplex-link $N $D 2Mb 1ms RED]
$ns simplex-link $D $N 1Mb 1ms DropTail
$ns queue-limit $N $D 50

# queue monitoring, RED
set redq [[$ns link $N $D] queue]
set traceq [open red-queue.tr w]
$redq trace curq_
$redq trace ave_
$redq attach $traceq

#Nodes and links
for {set j 1} {$j<=$NodeNb} { incr j } {
```

```
    set S($j) [$ns node]
    $ns duplex-link $S($j) $N 100Mb 1ms DropTail
    $ns queue-limit $S($j) $N 100
}
# set flow monitor
set monfile [open mon.tr w]
set fmon [$ns makeflowmon Fid]
$ns attach-fmon $flink $fmon
$fmon attach $monfile

#TCP Sources, destinations, connections
for {set i 1} {$i<=$NodeNb} { incr i } {
   for {set j 1} {$j<=$NumberFlows} { incr j } {
       set tcpsrc($i,$j) [new Agent/TCP/Newreno]
       set tcp_snk($i,$j) [new Agent/TCPSink]
       set k [expr $i*1000 +$j];
       $tcpsrc($i,$j) set fid_ $k
       $tcpsrc($i,$j) set window_ 2000
       $ns attach-agent $S($i) $tcpsrc($i,$j)
       $ns attach-agent $D $tcp_snk($i,$j)
       $ns connect $tcpsrc($i,$j) $tcp_snk($i,$j)
       set ftp($i,$j) [$tcpsrc($i,$j) attach-source FTP]
} }
# Generators for random size of files.
set rng1 [new RNG]
set rng2 [new RNG]

for { set i 0 } {$i<$rep } {incr i } {
   $rng1 next-substream;
   $rng2 next-substream;
}
# Random inter-arrival times of TCP transfer at each source i
set RV [new RandomVariable/Exponential]
$RV set avg_ 0.3
$RV use-rng $rng1

# Random size of files to transmit
set RVSize [new RandomVariable/Pareto]
$RVSize set avg_ 10000
$RVSize set shape_ 1.5
$RVSize use-rng $rng2
```

```
# We now define the beginning times of transfers and the transfer sizes
# Arrivals of sessions follow a Poisson process.
for {set i 1} {$i<=$NodeNb} { incr i } {
     set t [$ns now]
     for {set j 1} {$j<=$NumberFlows} { incr j } {
          # set the beginning time of next transfer from source and attributes
          set t [expr $t + [$RV value]]
          $tcpsrc($i,$j) set starts $t
          $tcpsrc($i,$j) set sess $j
          $tcpsrc($i,$j) set node $i
          $tcpsrc($i,$j) set size [expr [$RVSize value]]
   $ns at [$tcpsrc($i,$j) set starts] "$ftp($i,$j) send [$tcpsrc($i,$j) set size]"
           # update the number of flows
          $ns at [$tcpsrc($i,$j) set starts] "countFlows $i 1"
}}


for {set j 1} {$j<=$NodeNb} { incr j } {
   set Cnts($j) 0
}
# The following procedure is called whenever a connection ends
Agent/TCP instproc done {} {
global tcpsrc NodeNb NumberFlows ns RV ftp Out tcp_snk RVSize
# print in $Out: node, session, start time,  end time, duration,
# trans-pkts, transm-bytes, retrans-bytes, throughput
  set duration [expr [$ns now] - [$self set starts] ]
  puts $Out "[$self set node] \t [$self set sess] \t [$self set starts] \t\
     [$ns now] \t $duration \t [$self set ndatapack_] \t\
     [$self set ndatabytes_] \t [$self set  nrexmitbytes_] \t\
     [expr [$self set ndatabytes_]/$duration ]"
  countFlows [$self set node] 0
}
# The following recursive procedure updates the number of connections
# as a function of time. Each 0.2 it prints them into $Conn. This
# is done by calling the procedure with the "sign" parameter equal
# 3 (in which case the "ind" parameter does not play a role). The
# procedure is also called by the "done" procedure whenever a connection
# from source i ends by assigning the "sign" parameter 0, or when
# it begins, by assigning it 1 (i is passed through the "ind" variable).
proc countFlows { ind sign } {
global Cnts Conn NodeNb
set ns [Simulator instance]
     if { $sign==0 } { set Cnts($ind) [expr $Cnts($ind) - 1]
```

```
} elseif { $sign==1 } { set Cnts($ind) [expr $Cnts($ind) + 1]
} else {
  puts -nonewline $Conn "[$ns now] \t"
  set sum 0
  for {set j 1} {$j<=$NodeNb} { incr j } {
    puts -nonewline $Conn "$Cnts($j) \t"
    set sum [expr $sum + $Cnts($j)]
  }
  puts $Conn "$sum"
  $ns at [expr [$ns now] + 0.2] "countFlows 1 3"
} }
proc finish {} {
        global ns tf
        $ns flush-trace
        close $tf
        exec grep  "a" red-queue.tr > ave.tr
        exec grep  "Q" red-queue.tr > cur.tr
        exit 0
}
$ns at 0.5 "countFlows 1 3"
$ns at [expr $sduration - 0.01] "$fmon dump"
$ns at $sduration "finish"
$ns run
```

The flow monitor file includes more detailed information on the drop type. It allows to distinguish between Early Drops (ED) due to early discard of packets, and actual drops due to buffer overflow. The file has the following format:

1. Column 1: the time at which "dump" was performed.

2. Columns 2 and 5: both give the flow id.

3. Column 3: null (a zero entry).

4. Column 4: flow type.

5. Columns 6 and 7: source and destination of the flow.

6. Columns 8 and 9: total number of arrivals of the flow in packets and in bytes, respectively.

7. Columns 10 and 11: amount of early drops of the flow in packets and in bytes, respectively.

8. Columns 12 and 13: total number of arrivals of all flows in packets and in bytes, respectively.

9. Columns 14 and 15: amount of early drops of all flows in packets and in bytes, respectively.

10. Columns 16 and 17: total amount of drops of all flows in packets and in bytes, respectively.

11. Columns 18 and 19: total amount of drops of the particular flow in packets and in bytes, respectively.

Note: in order to apply the flow monitor, each TCP connection that we wish to monitor should have a flow id. In our case, we initially identify a flow by its number and its source node (e.g., the third TCP connection that starts at node 4). We transform this into a one dimensional vector as follows:

```
set k [expr $i*1000 +$j];
$tcpsrc($i,$j) set fid_ $k
```

The simulation produced the following output files:

1. cur.tr and ave.tr that monitor the evolution of the queue size and its averaged version.

2. Conn.tr for monitoring the number of active connections from each of the six sources (the number six is given as parameter in the script to the variable NumberFlows) as well as the sum of active sessions, as a function of time.

3. Out.ns for monitoring for each session (identified with the source node and the session number originating from that node), start time, end time and duration of the connection, the number of transmitted packets, transmitted bytes and retransmitted bytes, and the throughput experienced by the session.

4. mon.tr is the trace produced by the flow monitor that contains number of transmitted packets and bytes and number of losses per connection.

5. out.tr is the global trace of all events.

We used in the above script the RED version with automatic configuration. We plot the queue size and its averaged dynamics in Figures 6.9-6.10. We see that the queue length process is much more bursty and variable than in the case of persistent TCP connections (which we saw in Figures 6.4 and 6.5). The number of active connection is given in Figure 6.11.

We included in the above script various ways of monitoring. The direct way of monitoring the number of retransmissions and arrivals of packets through the procedure "done" has the advantage that it is global: it gives all the data related to the connection. The flow monitor gives on the other hand local information on losses at a particular link. If the connection traverses several bottleneck links, the first method is thus more advantageous. The second method has the advantage of giving more detailed local information which can be useful to understand the contribution of each of several nodes to congestion suffered by a session.

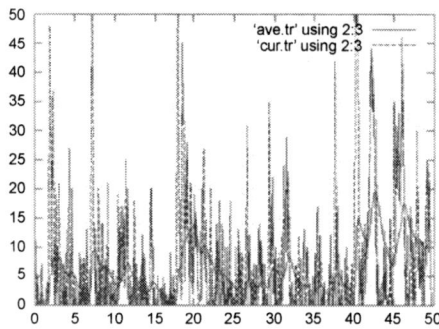

Figure 6.9: Evolution of the queue size and of its average.

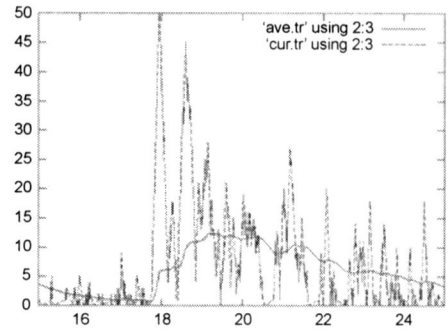

Figure 6.10: Queue size and averaged size evolution: a zoom.

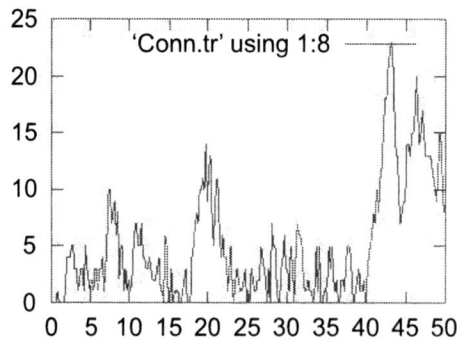

Figure 6.11: Number of active connections as a function of time.

6.5   EXERCISES

6.1. Consider the script shortRed.tcl (Listing 6.3) and modify the program to have manual adjustment of the parameters `thresh_`, `maxthresh_`, `q_weight_`. How should these parameters, as well as the queue size on link N-D be chosen so as to maximize the throughput? Study this by simulation and explain the tradeoffs.

6.2. One of the objectives of RED is to allow more fairness to short bursts. Analyze the throughput and the loss probability of a connection as a function of its size with RED and compare it to Drop-Tail. Use the script shortRed.tcl (Table 6.3). Try various parameters for RED to get better fairness. The exercise is based on [10].

CHAPTER 7

Differentiated Services

In traditional Internet, all connections get the same treatment in the network. This is in contrast with other networking concepts, such as the ATM (Asynchronous Transfer Mode), that can offer quality of service requirements to connections at the price of much higher signalling and processing related to the acceptance of new connections and maintaining the guarantees of ongoing connections. Moreover, since network resources are limited, offering guarantees on performance measures requires rejecting new connections if resources are not available. This is in contrast with the best effort characteristic of today's Internet where no admission control is performed.

Yet, it has been recognized that it is important to differentiate between connection classes and to be able to allocate resources to connections according to their class. Thus a subscriber that is willing to pay more could benefit by smaller delays and larger throughputs. This is of interest in particular for real time applications over the Internet (voice, video).

For that reason, the Diffserv has been introduced. It is based on marking packets at the edge of the network according to the performance level that the network wishes to provide them; then according to the marks, the packets are treated differently at the network's nodes. A common way to differentiate packets is by using RED buffers with different parameters for different packets.

The NS-2 module that handles diffserv has been developed in Nortel Networks, and this Chapter is based in large part on the excellent Nortel Report [48].

7.1   DESCRIPTION OF ASSURED FORWARDING DIFFSERV

The Diffserv implemented in NS-2 follows the "Assured forwarding" approach standardized in [32]. A packet belonging to a flow may receive three possible priority levels within the flow. These are called sometime "drop precedences". This can be used, for example to provide a lower loss probability to sync packets in a TCP connection, since unlike other packets, the losses of sync packets result in very long time-outs [8]. In addition to differentiation within each flow, all flows are classified into several classes (at most four), and different treatment can be given to the different classes.

Moreover, it is possible to differentiate between flows. Four classes of flows are defined, and packets of a given class are queued in a class-dependent queue. In order to differentiate between packets belonging to the same class, three virtual queues are implemented in each of the four queues. To each of the 12 combinations of the four flow class and the three internal priority levels within a flow, there corresponds a code point that a packet is given when entering the network. In practice not all queues and all priority groups need to be implemented.

Diffserv architecture has three components:

1. Policy and resource manager: it creates policies and distributes them to diffserv routers. A policy determines which level of services in the network are assigned to which packets. This assignment may depend on the behavior of the source of the flow (e.g., its average rate and its burstiness) and special network elements are therefore added at the edge of the network in order to measure the source behavior. In ns simulation, the policy is fully determined in the tcl script.

2. Edge routers: are responsible for assigning the code points to the packets according to the policy specified by the network administrator. To do so they measure parameters of the input traffic of each flow.

3. Core routers: the basic approach of diffserv is to keep the intelligence in the edge of the network; routers within the network have simply to assign the appropriate priority to packets according to their code mark. The priority translates to parameters of the scheduling and to the dropping decisions in the core routers.

7.2   MRED ROUTERS

7.2.1   GENERAL DESCRIPTION

The fact that there are three virtual RED buffers (called MRED - Multi RED) in each physical queue allows the ability to enhance its behavior and to create dependence between their operation. One way to do that is through the RIO C (Rio Coupled) version of MRED, in which the probability of dropping low priority packets (called "out-of-profile packets") is based on the weighted average lengths of all virtual queues, whereas the probability of dropping a high priority ("in-profile") packet is based only on the weighted average length of its own virtual queue.

In contrast, in RIO-D (RIO De-coupled) the probability of dropping each packet is based on the size of its virtual queue. Another version is the WRED (Weighted Red) in which all probabilities are based on a single queue length [18]. It is possible to use also the dropTail queue.

7.2.2   CONFIGURATION OF MRED IN NS-2

To determine the number of physical queues, we use the command

```
$dsredq set numQueues_ $m
```

where m can take values between 1 and 4.

Configuring queue 0 to be a RIO-C is done with the command

```
$dsredq setMREDMode RIO-C 0
```

If the last argument is not given then all queues are set to be RIO-C. Similarly, types other than RIO-C can be defined. To specify the number $n of virtual queues, we use the command

```
$dsredq setNumPrec $n
```

Red parameters are then configured using the command

```
$dsredq configQ $queueNum $virtualQueueNum $minTh $maxTh $maxP
```

It thus has 5 parameters: the queue number, virtual queue number, min_{th}, max_{th} and max_p. The parameter q_w can also be given (as the 6th parameter) and if it is not stated then it is taken to be 0.002 by default.

The droptail queue can also be used with the command

```
$dsredq setMREDMode DROP
```

The configuation then is given as before with only the first three parameters:

```
$dsredq configQ $queueNum $virtualQueueNum $minTh
```

All arriving packets are dropped when the min_{th} value is reached.

As we saw in the chapter on RED, for computing the drop probability we need an estimate of the packet size. For a packet of size 1000 bytes this is given by the command

```
$dsredq meanPktSize 1000
```

Scheduling Particular scheduling regimes can be defined, for example the weighted round robin (WRR) with queue weights 5 and 1, respectively, will be defined through

```
$dsredq setSchedularMode WRR
$dsredq addQueueWeights 1 5
```

Other possible scheduling are Weighted Interleaved Round Robin (WIRR), Round Robin (RR), which is the default scheduling, and the strict priorities (PRI).

PHB table The set of four queues along with the virtual queues is implemented with a PHB (Per Hop Behavior) table. Its entries are defined by (i) the code point (ii) the class (physical queue) and (iii) the "precedence" (virtual queue). An entry is assigned with the command of the form

```
$dsredq addPHBEntry 11 0  1
```

which means that code point 11 is mapped to the virtual queue 1 of the physical queue 0.

7.2.3 TCL QUERYING

The following three commands result in printing respectively (i) the PHB table, (ii) the number of physical and virtual queues and (iii) the RED weighted average size of the specified physical queues (0 in our case):

```
$dsredq printPHBTable
$dsredq printStats
$dsredq getAverage 0
```

7.3   DEFINING POLICIES

7.3.1   DESCRIPTION

All flows having the same source and destination are subject to a common policy. A policy defines a policer type, a target rate, and other policy specific parameters. It specifies at least two code points. The choice between them depends on the comparison between the flow's target and its current sending rate, and possibly on the policy-dependent parameters (such as burstiness). The policy specifies meter types that are used for measuring the relevant input traffic parameters. A packet arriving at the edge device causes the meter to update the state variables corresponding to the flow, and the packet is then marked according to the policy. The packet has an initial code point corresponding to the required service level; the marking can result in downgrading the service level with respect to the initial required one.

A policy table is used in NS-2 to store the policy type of each flow. Not all entries are actually used. The entries are

1. Source node ID

2. Destination node ID

3. Policer type

4. Meter type

5. Initial code point

6. CIR (committed information rate)

7. CBS (committed burst size)

8. C bucket (current size of the committed bucket)

9. EBS (excess burst size)

10. E bucket (current size of the excess bucket)

11. PIR (peak information rate)

12. PBS (peak burst size)

13. P bucket (current size of the peak bucket)

14. Arrival time of last packet

15. Average sending rate

16. TSW window length (TSW is a policer based on average transmission rates and the averaging is performed over the window length, in seconds, of data). The default value is 1 sec.

The following are the possible policer types:

1. **TSW2CM (TSW2CMPolicer):** uses a CIR and two drop precedences. The lower one is used probabilistically when the CIR is exceeded.

2. **TSW3CM (TSW3CMPolicer)** [26]: uses a CIR, a PIR and three drop precedences. The medium priority level is used probabilistically when the CIR is exceeded, and the lowest one is used probabilistically when the PIR is exceeded.

3. **Token Bucket (TokenBucketPolicer)**: uses CIR and a CBS, and two drop precedences.

4. **Single Rate Three Color Marker (srTCMPolicer)** [33]: uses CIR, CBS and EBS to choose from three drop precedences.

5. **Two Rate Three Color Marker (trTCMPolicer)** [33]: uses CIR, CBS, EBS and PBS to choose from three drop precedences.

Each of the above policer type defines the meter it uses. A policer table defines for each policy type the initial code point as well as one or two downgraded code points. The initial code point is often called "green code" and the lowest downgraded code is "red". If there is another code point in between, it is called "yellow".

7.3.2 CONFIGURATION

To update the policy table, the "addPolicyEntry" command is used, which contains the edge queue variable denoting the edge queue, the source and destination nodes of the flow, the policer type, its initial code point, and then the values of the parameters that it uses; these are some or all of CIR, CBS, PIR and PBS as stated above. CIR and PIR are given in bps, and CBS, EBS and PBS in bytes. An example is:

```
$edgeQueue addPolicerEntry [$n1 id] [$n8 id] trTCM 10 200000 1000 300000 1000
```

Here we added a policy for the flow that originates in $n1 and ends at $n8. If the TSW policers are used, one can add at the end the TSW window length. If not added, it is taken to be 1 sec by default.

Then another "addPolicyEntry" command specific to the policy and to the initial code point (and not to a particular flow) defines the downgraded code points which are common to all flows that use the policy with the same initial code point. An example is:

```
$edgeQueue addPolicerEntry srTCM 10 11 12
```

7.3.3 TCL QUERYING

The following three commands result in printing respectively (i) the entire policy table, (ii) the entire policer table and (iii) the current size in bytes of the C buckets:

```
$edgeQueue printPolicyTable
$edgeQueue printPolicerTable
$edgeQueue getBucket
```

7.4 SIMULATION OF DIFFSERV: PROTECTION OF VULNERABLE PACKETS

In TCP connections, the loss of some segments has more impact than others on the performance of the connection. These segments are (i) the connection establishment segments, (ii) the segments sent when the connection has a small window, and (iii) the segments sent after a timeout or a fast retransmit. We call these "vulnerable" segments, or packets. In a Infocom paper [43], the authors show that by marking these segments with a higher priority and implementing the priority using a diffserv architecture, the performance of the TCP connection considerably improves. This marking requires, however, that network layer elements be aware of transport layer information, i.e., of the state of the TCP connection. The goal of the simulation example we introduce is to show that one can achieve prioritization of sensitive segments without any use of transport layer information, thus simplifying the implementation of diffserv marking of TCP packets. This part is based on [8].

7.4.1 THE SIMULATED SCENARIO

Preliminaries on the service differentiation Two priority levels are defined: the higher "In packets" or "green packets" and the lower "Out packets" or "red packets". We focus on the simplest policer available in ns: the time-sliding window (TSW2CM). A CIR is defined for each edge router. As long as the connection's rate is below CIR, all packets are marked as high priority. When the rate exceeds CIR, packets are marked probabilistically such that on the average, the rate of packets marked with high priority corresponds to the CIR. The transmitted rate is computed as the rate averaged over the "TSW window"; in our simulation its duration is 20 msec.

In our experimentations we vary the CIR level at the source edge nodes and study its impact on performance.

The topology We consider the simple network topology with a single bottleneck, depicted in Figure 7.1.

Each source node is connected to a corresponding edge node where the traffic is marked according to parameters that will be specified. The edge routers are connected to a bottleneck corerouter, and then through another edge router, to a destination node.

There are 20 source nodes, and each one of them generates TCP connections.

We experiment with a high-speed local area type network (short propagation delays) with completely symmetric links:

- Links between the edge nodes and the corresponding source nodes have delays of 10 μsec and 6Mbps bandwidth.

- Links between the edge node and the corresponding destination node has 10 μsec delay and 10Mbps bandwidth.

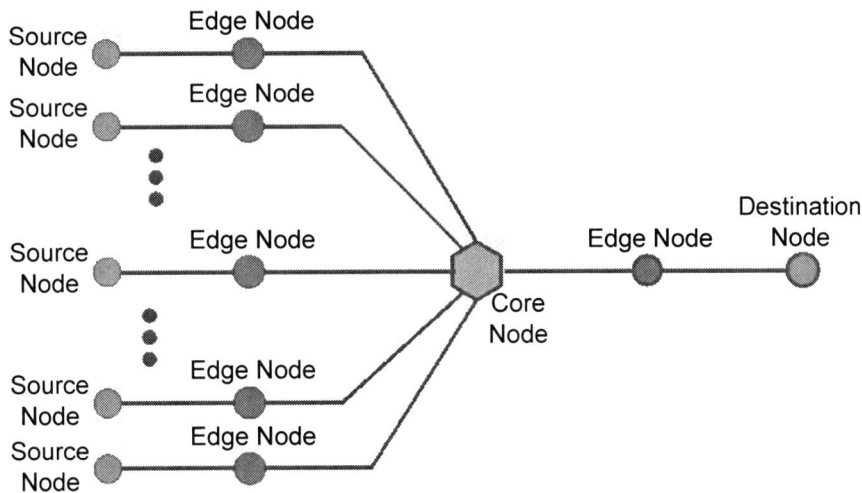

Figure 7.1: Network topology.

- Links between the core node and edge nodes that are attached to the sources have 0.1msec delay and 6Mbps bandwidth.

- The link between the core node and edge node attached to the destination has 1msec delay and 10Mbps bandwidth.

The traffic model   The size of a transferred file has a Pareto distribution with shape parameter 1.25 and an average size of 10kbytes (see [14, 54] for similar parameters).

Files to be transmitted arrive at each source node according to a Poisson process with an average rate of 5 files per second. Several sessions from the same source node can be active simultaneously.

Queueing management parameters   A queue can build up only at the bottleneck router, i.e., at the link between the core node and the edge node that connects to the destination. We chose its size to be of 100 packets. Thus the queue management parameters at other nodes did not have an influence on the results. In the bottleneck queue at the core node, a multi-RED queue management is used with a RIO-D version; we choose the same parameters for both priority levels (more details will be given below). Our aim in choosing the parameters was not to obtain necessarily an optimal performance but rather to create conditions that allow us to study the effect of diffserv on diminishing the loss probabilities of vulnerable segments, and the impact of this action on TCP performance (delay, throughput). For that reason, we choose the same parameters for the two priority levels (this will be explained below).

For each color of packets (red, green), the averaged queue sized is monitored (this is done using the standard exponential averaging with parameter $w_q = 0.01$). Packets of a given color start to be dropped when the averaged number of queued packets of this color exceeds min_w; we choose

$min_w = 15$; this drop probability increases linearly with the averaged queue size until it reaches the value $max_w = 45$, where the drop probability is taken to be $max_p = 0.5$. When this value is exceeded, the drop probability is 1.

Note that often the differentiation between the priorities is done using different sets of parameters: drops are performed at a larger queue size for green packets (e.g., [52]). We prefer not to use this approach, since with rejection at a larger window size we also get larger delays, which in some experimented parameters result in a lower throughput for green packets than for red packets and in global degradation of performance. By giving the same parameters to both priorities, we can learn about the direct effect of protecting vulnerable packets on the TCP performance. The differentiation is then done by using the RIO-D approach, in which the rejection probability of each type of color depends on the average number of packets of that type. Thus to have green packets dropped less than red ones, we simply choose their throughput (and consequently also the corresponding average queue size) to be lower; this is done by the proper choice of the CIR value which determines the fraction of packets that will be marked green.

Simulations are 80 sec long. This is a very short simulation time, but we use it only as an example, in a realistic simulation study one needs to simulate till the confidence interval specified will be achieved.

The rate of arrival of bits to the bottleneck is

$$\frac{20 \times 1.04 \times 10^4 \times 8}{0.22} = 7.563 Mbps$$

This is obtained as follows: An average packet size is 1040 bytes of which 1000 are data and 40 bytes are an extra header. An average ftp file is assumed to contain 10^4 bytes of data, which means that its total average size (including the extra headers) is approximately $1.04 \times 10^4 \times 8$ bits. The result is obtained by multiplying by the number of source nodes and dividing by the average time between arrivals of files at a node.

The NS-2 script is given in Listing 7.1.

Listing 7.1: Tcl script diffs.tcl.

```
set ns [new Simulator]


# There are several sources each generating many TCP sessions sharing a bottleneck
# link and a single destination. Their number is given by the parameter NodeNb

#      S(1) ----- E(1) ----
#      .                  |
#      .         ---- E(i) ---Core---- Ed -------- D
#      .                  |
#      S(NodeNb)- E(NodeNb)-
```

```
set cir0        100000; # policing parameter
set cir1        100000; # policing parameter
set pktSize     1000
set NodeNb       20; # Number of source nodes
set NumberFlows 360 ; # Number of flows per source node
set sduration    80  ; # Duration of simulation
set run           1; #simulation run

#Define different colors for data flows (for NAM)
$ns color 1 Blue
$ns color 2 Red
$ns color 3 Green
$ns color 4 Brown
$ns color 5 Yellow
$ns color 6 Black

set Out [open Out.ns w];   # file containing transfer
                           # times of different connections
set Conn [open Conn.tr w]; # file containing the number of connections

set tf   [open out.tr w];  # Open the Trace file
$ns trace-all $tf

#Open the NAM trace file
set file2 [open out.nam w]
# $ns namtrace-all $file2

# defining the topology
set D    [$ns node]
set Ed   [$ns node]
set Core [$ns node]

set flink [$ns simplex-link $Core $Ed 10Mb 1ms dsRED/core]
$ns queue-limit  $Core $Ed   100
$ns simplex-link $Ed $Core 10Mb 1ms dsRED/edge
$ns duplex-link  $Ed    $D  10Mb    0.01ms DropTail

for {set j 1} {$j<=$NodeNb} { incr j } {
 set S($j) [$ns node]
 set E($j) [$ns node]
 $ns duplex-link  $S($j) $E($j)  6Mb    0.01ms DropTail
```

```
 $ns simplex-link $E($j) $Core    6Mb    0.1ms dsRED/edge
 $ns simplex-link $Core  $E($j)   6Mb    0.1ms dsRED/core
 $ns queue-limit $S($j) $E($j) 100
}


#Config Diffserv
set qEdC     [[$ns link $Ed $Core] queue]
$qEdC        meanPktSize 40
$qEdC    set numQueues_    1
$qEdC      setNumPrec      2
for {set j 1} {$j<=$NodeNb} { incr j } {
 $qEdC addPolicyEntry [$D id] [$S($j) id] TSW2CM 10 $cir0 0.02
}
$qEdC addPolicerEntry TSW2CM 10 11
$qEdC addPHBEntry  10 0 0
$qEdC addPHBEntry  11 0 1
$qEdC configQ 0 0 10 30 0.1
$qEdC configQ 0 1 10 30 0.1


$qEdC printPolicyTable
$qEdC printPolicerTable

set qCEd     [[$ns link $Core $Ed] queue]
# set qCEd     [$flink queue]
$qCEd       meanPktSize $pktSize
$qCEd set numQueues_    1
$qCEd set NumPrec        2
$qCEd addPHBEntry  10 0 0
$qCEd addPHBEntry  11 0 1
$qCEd setMREDMode RIO-D
$qCEd configQ 0 0 15 45   0.5 0.01
$qCEd configQ 0 1 15 45   0.5 0.01

for {set j 1} {$j<=$NodeNb} { incr j } {
 set qEC($j) [[$ns link $E($j) $Core] queue]
 $qEC($j) meanPktSize $pktSize
 $qEC($j) set numQueues_    1
 $qEC($j) setNumPrec        2
 $qEC($j) addPolicyEntry [$S($j) id] [$D id] TSW2CM 10 $cir1 0.02
 $qEC($j) addPolicerEntry TSW2CM 10 11
 $qEC($j) addPHBEntry  10 0 0
 $qEC($j) addPHBEntry  11 0 1
```

```
# $qEC($j) configQ 0 0 20 40 0.02
 $qEC($j) configQ 0 0 10 20 0.1
 $qEC($j) configQ 0 1 10 20 0.1


$qEC($j) printPolicyTable
$qEC($j) printPolicerTable


 set qCE($j) [[$ns link $Core $E($j)] queue]
 $qCE($j) meanPktSize       40
 $qCE($j) set numQueues_     1
 $qCE($j) setNumPrec        2
 $qCE($j) addPHBEntry   10 0 0
 $qCE($j) addPHBEntry   11 0 1
# $qCE($j) configQ 0 0 20 40 0.02
 $qCE($j) configQ 0 0 10 20 0.1
 $qCE($j) configQ 0 1 10 20 0.1
}


# set flow monitor
set monfile [open mon.tr w]
set fmon [$ns makeflowmon Fid]
$ns attach-fmon $flink $fmon
$fmon attach $monfile


#TCP Sources, destinations, connections
for {set i 1} {$i<=$NodeNb} { incr i } {
for {set j 1} {$j<=$NumberFlows} { incr j } {
set tcpsrc($i,$j) [new Agent/TCP/Newreno]
set tcp_snk($i,$j) [new Agent/TCPSink]
set k [expr $i*1000 +$j];
$tcpsrc($i,$j) set fid_ $k
$tcpsrc($i,$j) set window_ 2000
$ns attach-agent $S($i) $tcpsrc($i,$j)
$ns attach-agent $D $tcp_snk($i,$j)
$ns connect $tcpsrc($i,$j) $tcp_snk($i,$j)
set ftp($i,$j) [$tcpsrc($i,$j) attach-source FTP]
} }


# Generators for random size of files.
set rng1 [new RNG]
set rng2 [new RNG]
for {set j 0} {$j < $run} {incr j} {
```

```
        $rng1 next-substream;
        $rng2 next-substream;
}


# Random inter-arrival times of TCP transfer at each source i
set RV [new RandomVariable/Exponential]
$RV set avg_ 0.22
$RV use-rng $rng1


# Random size of files to transmit
set RVSize [new RandomVariable/Pareto]
$RVSize set avg_ 10000
$RVSize set shape_ 1.25
$RVSize use-rng $rng2


# We now define the beginning times of transfers and the transfer sizes
# Arrivals of sessions follow a Poisson process.
#
for {set i 1} {$i<=$NodeNb} { incr i } {
     set t [$ns now]
     for {set j 1} {$j<=$NumberFlows} { incr j } {
         # set the beginning time of next transfer from source and attributes
         $tcpsrc($i,$j) set sess $j
         $tcpsrc($i,$j) set node $i
         set t [expr $t + [$RV value]]
         $tcpsrc($i,$j) set starts $t
         $tcpsrc($i,$j) set size [expr [$RVSize value]]
   $ns at [$tcpsrc($i,$j) set starts] "$ftp($i,$j) send [$tcpsrc($i,$j) set size]"
   $ns at [$tcpsrc($i,$j) set starts ] "countFlows $i 1"
}}


for {set j 1} {$j<=$NodeNb} { incr j } {
set Cnts($j) 0
}


# The following procedure is called whenever a connection ends
Agent/TCP instproc done {} {
global tcpsrc NodeNb NumberFlows ns RV ftp Out tcp_snk RVSize
# print in $Out: node, session, start time,  end time, duration,
# trans-pkts, transm-bytes, retrans-bytes, throughput
  set duration [expr [$ns now] - [$self set starts] ]
  set i [$self set node]
```

```
   set j [$self set sess]
   set time [$ns now]

   puts $Out "$i \t $j \t $time \t\
      $time \t $duration \t [$self set ndatapack_] \t\
      [$self set ndatabytes_] \t [$self set  nrexmitbytes_] \t\
      [expr [$self set ndatabytes_]/$duration ]"
          # update the number of flows
      countFlows [$self set node] 0
}


# The following recursive procedure updates the number of connections
# as a function of time. Each 0.2 it prints them into $Conn. This
# is done by calling the procedure with the "sign" parameter equal
# 3 (in which case the "ind" parameter does not play a role). The
# procedure is also called by the "done" procedure whenever a connection
# from source i ends by assigning the "sign" parameter 0, or when
# it begins, by assigning it 1 (i is passed through the "ind" variable).
#
proc countFlows { ind sign } {
global Cnts Conn NodeNb
set ns [Simulator instance]
      if { $sign==0 } { set Cnts($ind) [expr $Cnts($ind) - 1]
} elseif { $sign==1 } { set Cnts($ind) [expr $Cnts($ind) + 1]
} else {
  puts -nonewline $Conn "[$ns now] \t"
  set sum 0
  for {set j 1} {$j<=$NodeNb} { incr j } {
    puts -nonewline $Conn "$Cnts($j) \t"
    set sum [expr $sum + $Cnts($j)]
  }
  puts $Conn "$sum"
  $ns at [expr [$ns now] + 0.2] "countFlows 1 3"
} }


#Define a 'finish' procedure
proc finish {} {
        global ns tf qsize qbw qlost file2
        $ns flush-trace
        close $file2
        exit 0
}
```

```
$ns at 0.5 "countFlows 1 3"
$ns at [expr $sduration - 0.01] "$fmon dump"
$ns at [expr $sduration - 0.001] "$qCEd printStats"
$ns at $sduration "finish"
$ns run
```

7.5   SIMULATION RESULTS

Losses   We check the influence of the CIR marking rate on the loss probabilities of the SYN packets and of the first data packet in a connection, as before.

CIR	10kbps	30kbps	100kbps	200kbps	300kbps	1Mbps	10Mbps
Lost SYN packets	120	95	53	45	17	78	114
First packets lost	125	119	90	56	37	73	115
Total losses	1699	1612	1476	1286	1088	1290	1577

Table 7.1: Protection of vulnerable packets as a function of CIR.

We see that we manage to decrease the losses of SYN packets by a factor of seven, and the losses of the first data packet of a connexion by a factor of around 3.4, both obtained at CIR of 300kbps.

Throughput and Goodput   The number of data packets that were successfully transmitted during the simulations was independent of the CIR: it was on the average 58285, with a standard deviation of 395 packets. This is due to the fact that the arrival rate of sessions does not depend on the CIR. In view of the low loss probabilities, the throughput too, is almost constant as a function of CIR.

The number of sessions   The total number of sessions as a function of time is given in Figure 7.2 for the CIR of 200kbps (the optimal) and for the case of no prioritization (CIR of 10Mbps). We see from the simulation result that our marking scheme with CIR of 300kbps gives a better performance: less number of active sessions are present under this marking. This is related to the fact that the session duration in our marking is shorter, as we show in the next section. Indeed, since the arrival rate of sessions is the same independently of CIR, the average number of session should be proportional to the average duration of a session (the proportionality factor being the arrival rate of sessions).

Session duration   In Table 7.2 we present the average duration of a session as a function the CIR.

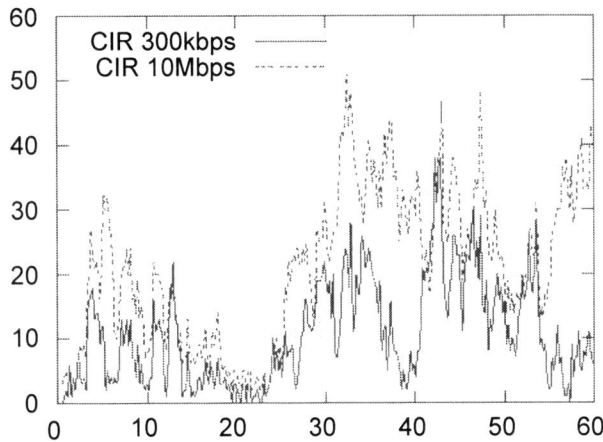

Figure 7.2: Evolution of total number of sessions.

CIR	10kbps	30kbps	100kbps	200kbps	300kbps	1Mbps	10Mbps
sess. duration	0.25261	0.23107	0.16794	0.14947	0.11950	0.20320	0.22507

Table 7.2: Average duration of a session as a function of CIR.

We see that in the range of 100kbps till 300kbps the average duration decreases by a factor between 1/3 (for 100kbps) and 1/2 (for 300kbps) with respect to the case of no prioritization.

7.6   DISCUSSIONS AND CONCLUSIONS

There are few limitation of the marking approach. The significant improvement that we obtain would not be obtained in any scenario, and we propose a few guidelines, which we validated through further simulations, to describe its limitations.

1. Vulnerable packets deteriorate performance considerably since they cause long timeouts. This is especially the case for the loss of a syn that results in a timeout of 3 sec or 6sec. In high speed networks the duration of a file transfer is short (often the whole transfer is much shorter than timeout), so we can expect to gain much by eliminating these long timeouts. In low speed networks, this is no longer the case so the gains in our approach become marginal.

2. In our simulation, an average file size is 10kbytes, which is the old averaged measured file size in the Internet [54]. This means that around 10% of the packets is a SYN packet, and furthermore, another 10% of the packets are first in a transfer. Thus in the absence of our approach, around 20% of lost packets would correspond to these types of vulnerable packets, so eliminating these losses can result in a considerable improvement in performance. If we

were to use our approach to much longer files, the fraction of vulnerable packets would be much smaller, so that the added value of our approach would be smaller.

7.7 EXERCISES

7.1. Our simulations have restricted to FTP type traffic. In this exercise we shall consider **HTTP type traffic:** The time between the end of transmission of a file till the beginning of the next transmission is exponentially distributed with a mean of 0.1 sec. This is called a "thinking time". Thus from each source node there can be only one file transmitted at the same time (at most one active session). Write a tcl program for this traffic model and check its performance as a function of the CIR. Compare with FTP type traffic.

CHAPTER 8

Mobile Networks and Wireless Local Area Networks

There are two approaches for wireless communication between two hosts. The first is the centralized cellular network in which each mobile is connected to one or more fixed base stations (each base station is responsible for a different cell), so that communication between two mobile stations requires the participation of one or more base stations. A second decentralized approach consists of an ad-hoc network between users who wish to communicate between each other. Due to the more limited range of a mobile terminal (with respect to a fixed base station), this approach requires mobile nodes not only to be sources or destination of packets but also to forward packets between other mobiles. Cellular stations have a much larger range than ad-hoc networks. However, ad-hoc networks have the advantage of being quickly deployable as they do not require an existing infrastructure.

In cellular networks, the wireless part is restricted only to access to a network, and within the networks classical routing protocols can be used. Ad-hoc networks, in contrast, rely on special routing protocols that have to be adapted to frequent topology changes.

To model cellular networks well, sophisticated simulation tools of the physical radio channel are often needed, as well as the simulation of power control mechanisms. NS-2 does not have an advanced physical layer module (although it contains some simple modeling features of radio channels).

In ad-hoc networks, in contrast, the routing protocols are central. ns allows to simulate the main existing routing as well as the transport and applications that use them. Moreover, it allows the ability to take into account the MAC and link layer, the mobility, and some basic features of the physical layer.

The current routing protocols implemented by NS-2 are

- DSDV - Destination Sequenced Distance Vector [47],

- DSR - Dynamic Source Routing [38],

- TORA/IMPE - Temporally Ordered Routing Algorithm / Internet MANET Encapsulation Protocol [19, 44, 45], and

- AODV - Ad-hoc On Demand Distance Vector [46].

8.1   THE ROUTING ALGORITHMS

There are several approaches in conventional routing algorithms in traditional wireline networks, and some ideas from these are also used in ad-hoc networks. Among the traditional approaches we shall mention the following:

1. **Link State.** Each node maintains a record of the complete topology with a cost per each link. Each node periodically broadcasts the link costs of its outgoing links to all other nodes using flooding. Each node updates its record of the network and applies a shortest path algorithm for choosing the next-hop for each destination.

2. **Distance Vector.** Each node only monitors the cost of its outgoing links. Instead of broadcasting the information to all nodes, it periodically broadcasts to each of its neighbors an estimate of the shortest distance to every other node in the network. The receiving nodes use this information to recalculate routing tables using a shortest path algorithm. This method is more computation efficient, easier to implement and requires less storage space than link state routing.

3. **Source routing.** Routing decisions are taken at the source, and packets carry along the complete path they should take.

4. **Flooding.** The source sends the information to all neighbors who continue sending it to their neighbors, etc. By using sequence numbers for the packets, a node is able to relay a packet only once.

Next we describe the Ad-hoc routing protocols implemented in ns.

8.1.1   DESTINATION SEQUENCED DISTANCE VECTOR - DSDV

DSDV is a distance vector routing protocol. Each node has a routing table that indicates for each destination, which is the next hop and number of hops to the destination. Each node periodically broadcasts routing updates. A sequence number is used to tag each route. It shows the freshness of the route: a route with higher sequence number is more favorable. In addition, among two routes with the same sequence number, the one with less hops is more favorable. If a node detects that a route to a destination has broken, then its hop number is set to infinity and its sequence number is updated (increased) but assigned an odd number: even numbers correspond to sequence numbers of connected paths.

8.1.2   AD-HOC ON DEMAND DISTANCE VECTOR - AODV

AODV is a distance vector type routing. It does not require nodes to maintain routes to destinations that are not actively used. As long as the endpoints of a communication connection have valid routes to each other, AODV does not intervene.

The protocol uses different messages to discover and maintain links: Route Requests (RREQs), Route Replies (RREPs), and Route Errors (RERRs). These message types are received via UDP, and normal IP header processing applies.

AODV uses a destination sequence number for each route entry. The destination sequence number is created by the destination for any route information it sends to requesting nodes. Using destination sequence numbers ensures loop freedom and allows to know which of several routes is "fresher". Given the choice between two routes to a destination, a requesting node always selects the one with the greatest sequence number.

When a node wants to find a route to another one, it broadcasts a RREQ to all the network till either the destination is reached or another node is found with a "fresh enough" route to the destination (a "fresh enough" route is a valid route entry for the destination whose associated sequence number is at least as great as that contained in the RREQ). Then a RREP is sent back to the source and the discovered route is made available.

Nodes that are part of an active route may offer connectivity information by broadcasting periodically local Hello messages (special RREP messages) to its immediate neighbors. If Hello messages stop arriving from a neighbor beyond some given time threshold, the connection is assumed to be lost.

When a node detects that a route to a neighbor node is not valid, it removes the routing entry and sends a RERR message to neighbors that are active and use the route; this is possible by maintaining active neighbor lists. This procedure is repeated at nodes that receive RERR messages. A source that receives an RERR can reinitiate a RREQ message.

AODV does not allow to handle unidirectional links.

8.1.3 DYNAMIC SOURCE ROUTING - DSR

Designed for mobile ad hoc networks with up to around two hundred nodes with possibly high mobility rate. The protocol works "on demand", i.e., without any periodic updates.

Packets carry along the complete path they should take. This reduces overheads for large routing updates at the network. The nodes store in their cache all known routes. The protocol is composed of route discovery and route maintenance.

At **route discovery**, a source requesting to send a packet to a destination broadcasts a Route Request (RREQ) packet. Nodes receiving RREQ search in their Route Cache for a route to the destination. If a route is not found then the RREQ is further transmitted and the node adds its own address to the recorded hop sequence. This continues till the destination or a node with a route to the destination is reached. The route back can be retrieved by the reverse hop record. As routes need not be symmetric, DSR checks the Route Cache of the replying node and if a route is found, it is used instead. Alternatively, one can piggyback the reply on a RREQ targeted at the originator. Hence unidirectional links can be handled.

Route maintenance: When originating or forwarding a packet using a source route, each node transmitting the packet is responsible for confirming that data can flow over the link from that node to the next hop. An acknowledgment can provide confirmation that a link is capable of carrying data. Acknowledgements are often already part of the MAC protocol in use (such as the link-layer acknowledgement frame defined by IEEE 802.11), or are "passive acknowledgement", i.e., a node knows that its packet is received by an intermediate node since it can hear that the intermediate node forwards it further. If such acknowledgements are not available then a node can request an acknowledgement (which can be sent directly to the source using another route). Acknowledgements may be requested several times (up to some given bound), and in the persistent absence of acknowledgement, the route is removed from the Route Cache and returns a "Route Error" to each node that has sent a packet routed over that link since an acknowledgement was last received. Nodes overhearing or forwarding packets should make use of all carried routing information to update its own Route Packet.

8.1.4   TEMPORALLY ORDERED ROUTING ALGORITHM - TORA

This protocol is of the family of link reversal protocols. It may provide several routes between a source and a destination. TORA contains three parts: creating, maintaining and erasing routes. At each node, a separate copy of TORA is run per each destination. TORA builds a directed acyclic graph rooted at the destination. It associates a height with each node in the network (with respect to a common destination). Messages flow from nodes with greater height to those with lower heights. Routes are discovered using Query (QRY) and Update (UPD) packets.

When a node with no downstream links needs a route to a destination, it broadcasts a QRY packet that propagates till it either finds a node with a route to the destination or the destination itself. That node will respond by broadcasting a UPD packet containing the node's height. A node receiving the UPD packet updates its height accordingly and broadcasts another UPD. This may result in a number of directed paths from the source to the destination.

If a node discovers a particular destination to be unreachable, it sets the corresponding local height to a maximum value. In case the node cannot find any neighbor with finite height w.r.t. this destination, it attempts to find a new route. In case there is no route to a destination (i.e., of a network partition), the node broadcasts a Clear (CLR) message resetting all routing states and removing invalid routes from its part of the network.

TORA operates on top of IMEP (Internet MANET Encapsulation Protocol) that provides reliable delivery of route-messages and that informs the routing protocol of changes of the links to its neighbors. IMEP tries to aggregate IMEP and TORA messages to a single packet (called block) so as to reduce overhead. To get information on the status of neighboring links, IMEP periodically sends BEACON messages answered by HELLO response messages.

8.2 SIMULATING MOBILE NETWORKS

8.2.1 SIMULATION SCENARIO

We start by presenting simple script that runs a single TCP connection over a 3-node network over an area of size 500m by 400m depicted in Figure 8.1. The location process is as follows.

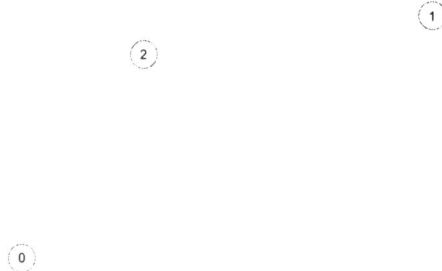

Figure 8.1: Example of a three node ad-hoc network.

- The initial locations of nodes 0, 1, and 2 are respectively (5,5), (490,285) and (150,240) (the z coordinate is assumed throughout to be 0).

- At time 10, node 0 starts moving towards point (250,250) at a speed of 3m/sec.
  At time 15, node 1 starts moving towards point (45,285) at a speed of 5m/sec.
  At time 10, node 0 starts moving towards point (480,300) at a speed of 5m/sec.
  Node 2 is still throughout the simulation.

The simulation lasts 150sec. At time 10, a TCP connection is initiated between node 0 and node 1. We shall use below the DSDV ad-hoc routing protocol and the IEEE802.11 MAC protocol.

8.2.2 WRITING THE TCL SCRIPT

We begin by specifying some basic parameters for the simulations, providing information for the different layers. This is done as follows:

```
set val(chan)          Channel/WirelessChannel   ;# channel type
set val(prop)          Propagation/TwoRayGround  ;# radio-propagation model
set val(netif)         Phy/WirelessPhy           ;# network interface type
set val(mac)           Mac/802_11                ;# MAC type
set val(ifq)           Queue/DropTail/PriQueue   ;# interface queue type
set val(ll)            LL                        ;# link layer type
set val(ant)           Antenna/OmniAntenna       ;# antenna model
set val(ifqlen)        50                        ;# max packet in ifq
set val(nn)            3                         ;# number of mobilenodes
```

```
set val(rp)              DSDV                    ;# routing protocol
set val(x)               500                     ;# X dimension of topography
set val(y)               400                     ;# Y dimension of topography
set val(stop)            150                     ;# time of simulation end
```

These parameters are used in the configuring of the nodes, which is done with the help of the following command

```
$ns node-config -adhocRouting $val(rp) \
                -llType $val(ll) \
                -macType $val(mac) \
                -ifqType $val(ifq) \
                -ifqLen $val(ifqlen) \
                -antType $val(ant) \
                -propType $val(prop) \
                -phyType $val(netif) \
                -channelType $val(chan) \
                -topoInstance $topo \
                -agentTrace ON \
                -routerTrace ON \
                -macTrace OFF \
                -movementTrace ON

     for {set i 0} {$i < $val(nn) } { incr i } {
             set node_($i) [$ns node]
     }
```

The four last options in the node-config can each be given a value of ON or OFF. The agentTrace will give in our case the trace of TCP, routerTrace provides tracing of packets involved in the routing, macTrace is related to tracing MAC protocol packets, and movementTrace is used to allow tracing the motion of nodes (for nam).

The initial location of node 0 is given as follows:

```
$node_(0) set X_ 5.0
$node_(0) set Y_ 5.0
$node_(0) set Z_ 0.0
```

and similarly we provide the initial location of other nodes.

A linear movement of a node is generated by specifying the time at which it starts, the x and y values of the target point and the speed. For example, the movement of node 1 will be written as

```
$ns at 15.0 "$node_(1) setdest 45.0 285.0 5.0"
```

We need to create the initial node position for nam using

```
for {set i 0} {$i < $val(nn)} { incr i } {
# 30 defines the node size for nam
$ns initial_node_pos $node_($i) 30
}
```

We tell nodes when the simulation ends with

```
for {set i 0} {$i < $val(nn) } { incr i } {
    $ns at $val(stop) "$node_($i) reset";
}
```

We then create the TCP connection and the ftp application over it as usual, see, e.g., Chapter 4. Ending the simulation is also as usual, except for an additional command for ending nam:

```
$ns at $val(stop) "$ns nam-end-wireless $val(stop)"
```

The complete trace of our program is given in Table 8.1.

8.3   TRACE FORMAT

An example of a line in the output trace is

```
r 40.639943289 _1_ AGT  --- 1569 tcp 1032 [a2 1 2 800] -------
    [0:0 1:0 32 1] [35 0] 2 0
```

- The first field is a letter that can have the values r,s,f,D for "received", "sent", "forwarded" and "dropped", respectively. It can also be M for giving a location or a movement indication, this is described later.

- The second field is the time.

- The third field is the node number.

- The fourth field is MAC to indicate if the packet refers to a MAC layer, it is AGT to indicate the transport layer (e.g., tcp) packet, or RTR if it refers to the routed packet. It can also be IFQ to indicate events related to the interference priority queue (like drop of packets).

- After the dashes come the global sequence number of the packet (this is not the tcp sequence number).

- At the next field comes more information on the packet type (e.g., tcp, ack or udp).

- Then comes the packet size in bytes.

- The 4 numbers in the first square brackets concern mac layer information. The first hexadecimal number, a2 (which equals 162 in decimal) specifies the expected time in seconds to send this data packet over the wireless channel. The second number, 1, stands for the MAC-id of the sending node, and the third, 2, is that of the receiving node. The fourth number, 800, specifies that the MAC type is ETHERTYPE_IP.

- The next numbers in the second square brackets refer to the IP source and destination addresses, then the ttl (Time To Live) of the packet (in our case 32).

- The third brackets concern the tcp information: its sequence number and the acknowledgement number.

There are other formats related to other routing mechanisms and/or packet types.

A movement command has the form:

```
M 10.00000 0 (5.00, 5.00, 0.00), (250.00, 250.00), 3.00
```

where the first number is the time, the second is the node number, then comes the origin and destination locations, and finally the speed is given.

Listing 8.1: Tcl script wrls-dsdv.tcl for TCP over an ad-hoc network.

```
# A 3-node example for ad-hoc simulation with DSDV

# Define options
set val(chan)         Channel/WirelessChannel    ;# channel type
set val(prop)         Propagation/TwoRayGround   ;# radio-propagation model
set val(netif)        Phy/WirelessPhy            ;# network interface type
set val(mac)          Mac/802_11                 ;# MAC type
set val(ifq)          Queue/DropTail/PriQueue    ;# interface queue type
set val(ll)           LL                         ;# link layer type
set val(ant)          Antenna/OmniAntenna        ;# antenna model
set val(ifqlen)       50                         ;# max packet in ifq
set val(nn)           3                          ;# number of mobilenodes
set val(rp)           DSDV                       ;# routing protocol
set val(x)            500                        ;# X dimension of topography
set val(y)            400                        ;# Y dimension of topography
set val(stop)         150                        ;# time of simulation end

set ns          [new Simulator]
set tracefd        [open simple.tr w]
set windowVsTime2 [open win.tr w]
set namtrace       [open simwrls.nam w]

$ns trace-all $tracefd
$ns namtrace-all-wireless $namtrace $val(x) $val(y)

# set up topography object
set topo        [new Topography]
```

```
$topo load_flatgrid $val(x) $val(y)


create-god $val(nn)


#
#  Create nn mobilenodes [$val(nn)] and attach them to the channel.
#
# configure the nodes
        $ns node-config -adhocRouting $val(rp) \
                        -llType $val(ll) \
                        -macType $val(mac) \
                        -ifqType $val(ifq) \
                        -ifqLen $val(ifqlen) \
                        -antType $val(ant) \
                        -propType $val(prop) \
                        -phyType $val(netif) \
                        -channelType $val(chan) \
                        -topoInstance $topo \
                        -agentTrace ON \
                        -routerTrace ON \
                        -macTrace OFF \
                        -movementTrace ON


        for {set i 0} {$i < $val(nn) } { incr i } {
                set node_($i) [$ns node]
        }

# Provide initial location of mobilenodes
$node_(0) set X_ 5.0
$node_(0) set Y_ 5.0
$node_(0) set Z_ 0.0

$node_(1) set X_ 490.0
$node_(1) set Y_ 285.0
$node_(1) set Z_ 0.0

$node_(2) set X_ 150.0
$node_(2) set Y_ 240.0
$node_(2) set Z_ 0.0

# Generation of movements
$ns at 10.0 "$node_(0) setdest 250.0 250.0 3.0"
```

```
$ns at 15.0 "$node_(1) setdest 45.0 285.0 5.0"
$ns at 110.0 "$node_(0) setdest 480.0 300.0 5.0"

# Set a TCP connection between node_(0) and node_(1)
set tcp [new Agent/TCP/Newreno]
$tcp set class_ 2
set sink [new Agent/TCPSink]
$ns attach-agent $node_(0) $tcp
$ns attach-agent $node_(1) $sink
$ns connect $tcp $sink
set ftp [new Application/FTP]
$ftp attach-agent $tcp
$ns at 10.0 "$ftp start"

# Printing the window size
proc plotWindow {tcpSource file} {
global ns
set time 0.01
set now [$ns now]
set cwnd [$tcpSource set cwnd_]
puts $file "$now $cwnd"
$ns at [expr $now+$time] "plotWindow $tcpSource $file" }
$ns at 10.1 "plotWindow $tcp $windowVsTime2"

# Define node initial position in nam
for {set i 0} {$i < $val(nn)} { incr i } {
# 30 defines the node size for nam
$ns initial_node_pos $node_($i) 30
}

# Telling nodes when the simulation ends
for {set i 0} {$i < $val(nn) } { incr i } {
    $ns at $val(stop) "$node_($i) reset";
}

# ending nam and the simulation
$ns at $val(stop) "$ns nam-end-wireless $val(stop)"
$ns at $val(stop) "stop"
$ns at 150.01 "puts \"end simulation\" ; $ns halt"
proc stop {} {
    global ns tracefd namtrace
    $ns flush-trace
```

```
    close $tracefd
    close $namtrace
}


$ns run
```

8.4   ANALYSIS OF SIMULATION RESULTS

At the beginning the nodes are too far away and a connection cannot be set. The first TCP signaling packet is transmitted at time 10 but the connection cannot be opened. Meanwhile nodes 0 and nodes 1 start moving towards node 2. After 6 seconds (timeout) a second attempt is made but still the connection cannot be established and the timeout value is doubled to 12sec. At time 28 another transmission attempt occurs. The timeout value is doubled again to 24 sec and again to 48 sec. Only at time 100 sec has the connection been established. The nodes 1 and 0 are close to each other so that a direct connection is established. The mobiles get further apart till the direct link breaks. The routing protocol is too slow to react and to create an alternative route. The window evolution is given in Figure 8.2 and a snap-shot of nam at time 124.15 sec is given in Figure 8.4.

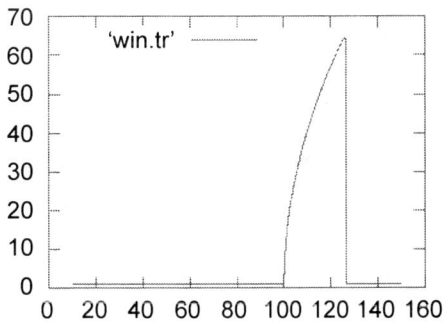

Figure 8.2: TCP window size in a three node scenario with DSDV routing protocol.

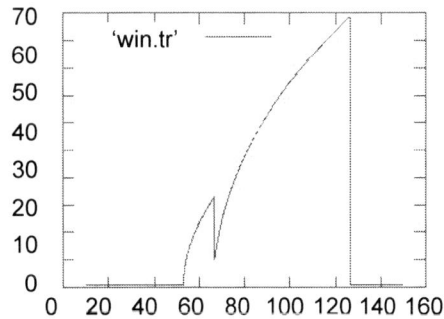

Figure 8.3: TCP window size in a three node scenario with DSDV routing protocol with both two and a single hop path.

Next we slightly change the parameters of the simulation. The only change is in fact that the ftp transfer will start now at time 12 instead of at time 10. This will cause both nodes 0 as well as node 1 to be within the radio range of node 2 when the timeout at around 53 sec expires so that when tcp connection is reattempted at that time a two hop path is established between node 0 and node 1. This is illustrated in Figure 8.5. At time 66 the nodes 0 and 1 are sufficiently close so a direct connection is established. The window size evolution is given in Figure 8.3. At the moment of the path change there is a single TCP packet loss that causes the window to decrease.

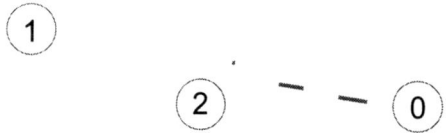

Figure 8.4: TCP in a three node scenario with DSDV routing protocol, time 124.14 sec, a single hop path.

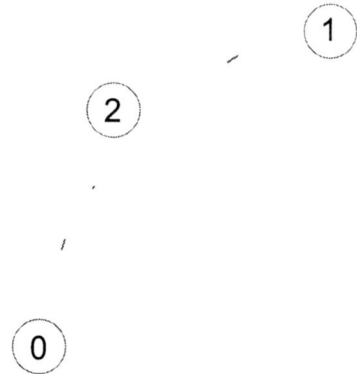

Figure 8.5: TCP in a three node scenario with DSDV routing protocol, time 58 sec: a 2 hop path.

At time 125.5 nodes 0 and 1 are too far apart for the connection to be maintained and the connection breaks.

8.5   COMPARISON WITH OTHER AD-HOC ROUTING

8.5.1   TCP OVER DSR

We first change the routing protocol to DSR by changing in wrls-dsdv.tcl the corresponding line to

```
set val(rp)   DSR   ;# routing protocol
```

When performing the simulation, we observe five phases of operation. In the first and last, the nodes are too far away and there is no connectivity. During phase 2 and 4, connection between nodes 0 and 1 use node 2 as a relay, whereas in the 3rd phase, there is a direct path between node 0 and 1.

Phase 2 starts at around time 40. Phase 3 starts at around 60 sec. At time 125.50 the fourth phase starts and at time 149 sec it ends, which ends the whole connection. This is described in Figure 8.6.

Here are some further observations:

- We note that in the DSDV, the system was not able to provide the 4th phase, so the connection was ended much earlier.

- The total number of TCP packets transferred using DSR is much larger than in DSDV. In DSR, 6770 TCP (data) packets have been received during the simulation, whereas in DSDV with the same parameters (corresponding to the script wrls-dsdv.tcl) it is 2079. (We can obtain this information by typing

```
grep "^r" simple.tr | grep "tcp" | grep "_1_ AGT" > tcp.tr
```

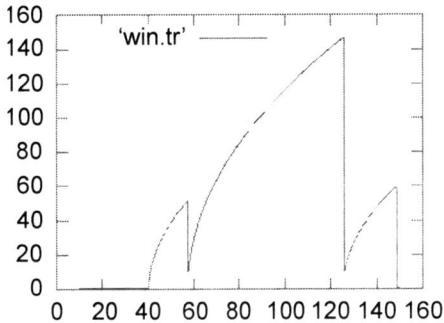

Figure 8.6: Window size evolution of the TCP connection for DSR.

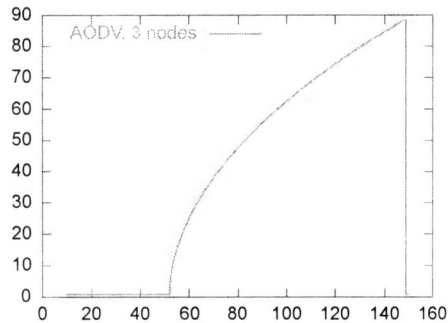

Figure 8.7: Window size evolution of the TCP connection for AODV.

and then counting the number of lines. Or we can be more precise and look at the sequence number of the last received tcp packet.)

If we follow the trace of a TCP packet, say the one with sequence number 6, we see that it appears at various times:

```
s 40.298003207 _0_ AGT   --- 1507 tcp 1040 [0 0 0 0] ...
r 40.298003207 _0_ RTR   --- 1507 tcp 1040 [0 0 0 0] ...
s 40.298003207 _0_ RTR   --- 1507 tcp 1060 [0 0 0 0] ...
f 40.310503613 _2_ RTR   --- 1507 tcp 1060 [13a 2 0 800] ...
r 40.310528613 _2_ RTR   --- 1507 tcp 1060 [13a 2 0 800] ...
f 40.310528613 _2_ RTR   --- 1507 tcp 1068 [13a 2 0 800] ...
r 40.348863637 _1_ RTR   --- 1507 tcp 1068 [13a 1 2 800] ...
r 40.348863637 _1_ AGT   --- 1507 tcp 1040 [13a 1 2 800] ...
```

It is first sent by the TCP agent at node 0, then received by the routing protocol of the same node and sent from there with an additional header. It is then received and forwarded by node 2, till finally it is received at node 1 at the routing level and then by the TCP agent. The above trace was obtained by enabling the tracing of agentTrace and routerTrace. Four other lines concerning the same packet will appear if we enable also the tracing of macTrace.

8.5.2   TCP OVER AODV

The simulations with the same parameters as before are repeated with AODV. The window size is given in Figure 8.7. The connection transferred altogether 3924 TCP data packets. It had throughout a long single phase in which the same two hop path was used, in which node 2 relayed the packets.

Due to the fact that changes in paths were avoided, there were no losses so the window remained high. However, we see that it reaches values less than DSR. This is due to the fact that the round trip time (needed to increase the window by one unit) is longer since a direct path is not used here. This explains the fact that it transfers less data during the simulation than DSR. We thus see that finding a shorter path results in a better TCP performance.

8.5.3   TCP OVER TORA

With the same parameters as in the previous simulations, i.e., wrls-dsdv.tcl, TORA gave no packet transfers at all! To increase connectivity, we added another fixed node at point (250,240) which only serves to relay packets. The window size evolution is given in Figure 8.8.

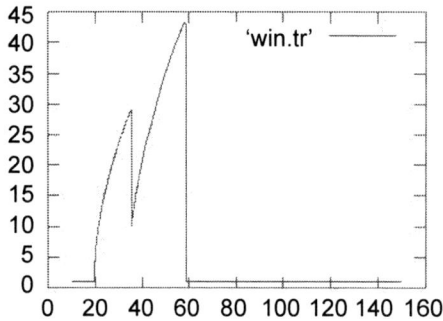

Figure 8.8: Window size of TCP over Tora with 4 nodes.

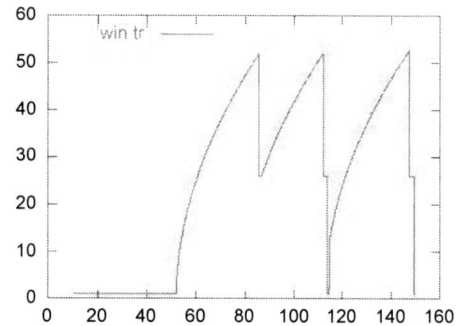

Figure 8.9: TCP over AODV with large value of maximum window.

We noted from the nam animation (or from the output trace) the following evolution. At the beginning there is no connectivity. When connectivity starts, a path is established using all nodes: 0-2-3-1 (see Figure 8.10 that describes the situation at time 33). At time 34.5sec a shorter forward path is established: 0-2-1, but the path of ACKs remains unchanged. Then at time 44 the ACK path changes to 1-3-0 (e.g., Figure 8.11).

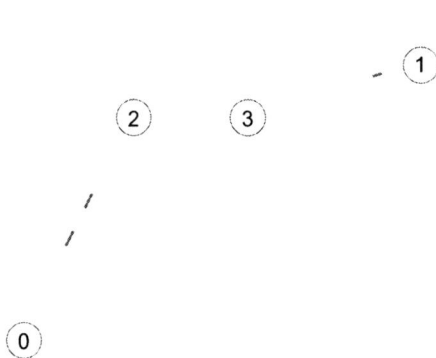

Figure 8.10: TCP over Tora with 4 nodes, time 33.

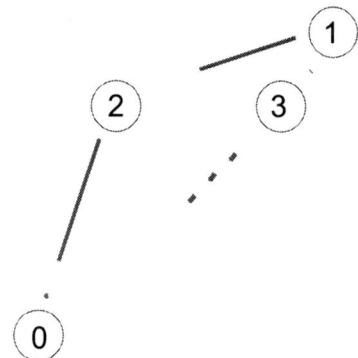

Figure 8.11: TCP over Tora with 4 nodes, time 56.

8.5.4   SOME COMMENTS

In the examples that we considered, losses occurred either when the geographical range was too large for reception or when there was a route change, and there were no losses due to buffer overflow. This is due to the fact that we used the default value of the maximum window size of TCP of 20. Thus the actual window that is used is the minimum between the congestion window and 20. In Figure 8.9 we present the window size evolution of TCP using AODV under the same conditions as those that were used to obtain Figure 8.7 but with a maximum window size of 2000. We see that we also obtain losses due to overflow.

8.6   THE INTERACTION OF TCP WITH THE MAC PROTOCOL

8.6.1   BACKGROUND

In the previous sections we considered a small number of mobiles, and saw how mobility phenomena influenced the performance of TCP. When there are a large number of terminals, particular new phenomena due to the MAC and physical layers may have a critical influence on TCP performance. To understand this interaction we first describe some aspects of the operation of the IEEE802.11 MAC layer and of the physical layer.

Each transmission of a DATA packet at the MAC level is part of a four-way handshake protocol. The mobile that wishes to send a packet, which we call M1, first sends an RTS (Request to Send) packet. If the destination mobile, which we call M2, can receive the packet, it sends a CTS (Clear to Send) packet. If M1 receives the CTS, it can then send the DATA packet (e.g., TCP data or ACK packet). Finally, M2 sends a (MAC layer) ACK so that M1 knows that the data packet has been well received.

This handshake protocol is intended to reduce the collision probability. Collisions may occur since a mobile, say M3, may wish to send a packet to M2 at the same time as M1 does; M3 may be out of range to sense the transmission from M1, so a collision of M1's and M3's packets may occur at M2. This phenomenon is called the "hidden terminal phenomenon". With the handshake protocol, M3 will not attempt to send any packet when it hears the CTS packet sent by M2 to M1.

If a sender M1 does not receive a CTS packet then it delays its transmission and makes later attempts to send a RTS. A sender drops the DATA packet if it has resent the RTS message seven times and has not heard a CTS reply from the receiver. A DATA packet is also dropped after four retransmissions without receiving a (MAC layer) ACK.

Although the handshake reduces the probability of "hidden terminal" collisions, it does not eliminate them. To understand how such collisions may occur, we should take into account the geographical range of interference and reception. Current hardware specifies that transmission range is about 250m and the carrier sensing range as well as the interference range are about 550m. Consider the chain topology in Figure 8.12, where the distance between nodes is 200m. Although nodes that are two hops apart are not hidden from each other, nodes that are three hops apart are, and may create collisions. Indeed, if node M4 wishes to send a packet to M5 during a transmission from node M1 to M2, it cannot hear the CTS from node M2 since it is out of the 250m range for good reception. It cannot hear M1's RTS or DATA packet since it is more than 550m away from M1. Therefore M4 may initiate transmission to M5 that will collide at node M2 with transmissions from M1. We shall study in this Section the impact of this type of collision on TCP performance using ns simulations, restricting to the chain topology. We shall not consider mobility aspects here. We refer to [9, 29, 55] for more details.

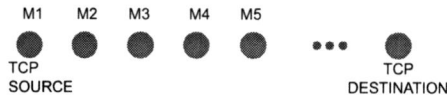

Figure 8.12: The chain topology.

The phenomenon that we have just described limits the number of packets that can be simultaneously transmitted in an ad-hoc network without collisions. This spatial constraint turns out to be the main factor limiting the performance of TCP in such environment and not buffer overflow. It is shown in [29] that for our chain topology, it is beneficial to limit the maximum window size of TCP to around $n/4$; further increase in the maximum window size causes more collisions and a deterioration of the throughput. In this section we shall check this assertion by simulations. Moreover, since the number of simultaneous packets that can be transmitted is limited, we shall try to improve TCP throughput by decreasing the ACK flows, using delayed ACK. ns allows us to simulate delayed ACKs with $d = 2$. We shall further show how to handle the case of $d > 2$ by making changes in NS-2 simulator.

8.6.2   THE SIMULATED SCENARIO

We use the standard two-ray ground propagation model, the IEEE802.11 MAC, and an omnidirectional antenna model of ns. We use the AODV routing algorithm, an interface queue length of 50 at each node We tested the NewReno version of TCP, which is the most deployed one. We tested four scenarios: 3, 9, 20 and 30 nodes. The cases of 3 and 9 nodes required 150 sec per simulation (to obtain stationary behavior). The other cases required 1500 sec per simulation. A TCP data packet is taken to be of size 1040 bytes (including the header). The script for the case of delayed ACK (with $d = 2$) is given in Table 8.2. Below, when configuring the nodes we shall use the option "macTrace ON" in order to have detailed tracing of MAC protocol packets. This will allow us to analyse the reason of each TCP packet loss that occurs.

Listing 8.2: Tcl script tcpwD.tcl for TCP over a static ad-hoc network with a chain topology.

```
# Define options
set val(chan)          Channel/WirelessChannel    ;# channel type
set val(prop)          Propagation/TwoRayGround    ;# radio-propagation model
```

```
set val(netif)        Phy/WirelessPhy           ;# network interface type
set val(mac)          Mac/802_11                ;# MAC type
set val(ifq)          Queue/DropTail/PriQueue   ;# interface queue type
set val(ll)           LL                        ;# link layer type
set val(ant)          Antenna/OmniAntenna       ;# antenna model
set val(ifqlen)       50                        ;# max packet in ifq
set val(nn)           9                         ;# number of mobilenodes
set val(rp)           AODV                      ;# routing protocol
set val(x)            2200                      ;# X dimension of topography
set val(y)             500                      ;# Y dimension of topography
set val(stop)         150               ;# time of simulation end


set ns          [new Simulator]
set tracefd     [open simple.tr w]
set windowVsTime2 [open win.tr w]


$ns trace-all $tracefd


# set up topography object
set topo        [new Topography]


$topo load_flatgrid $val(x) $val(y)


create-god $val(nn)


#
#   Create nn mobilenodes [$val(nn)] and attach them to the channel.
#


# configure the nodes
        $ns node-config -adhocRouting $val(rp) \
                        -llType $val(ll) \
                        -macType $val(mac) \
                        -ifqType $val(ifq) \
                        -ifqLen $val(ifqlen) \
                        -antType $val(ant) \
                        -propType $val(prop) \
                        -phyType $val(netif) \
                        -channelType $val(chan) \
                        -topoInstance $topo \
                        -agentTrace ON \
                        -routerTrace ON \
```

```
                          -macTrace ON \
                          -movementTrace OFF


        for {set i 0} {$i < $val(nn) } { incr i } {
                set node_($i) [$ns node]
        }


# Provide initial location of mobilenodes

for {set i 0} {$i < $val(nn)} { incr i } {
$node_($i) set X_ [expr ($i+1)*200.0]
$node_($i) set Y_ 250.0
$node_($i) set Z_ 0.0
}


# Set a TCP connection between node_(0) and node_(8)
set tcp [new Agent/TCP/Newreno]
$tcp set class_ 2
$tcp set  window_ 2000
Agent/TCPSink/DelAck set interval_ 100ms
set sink [new Agent/TCPSink/DelAck]
$ns attach-agent $node_(0) $tcp
$ns attach-agent $node_(8) $sink
$ns connect $tcp $sink
set ftp [new Application/FTP]
$ftp attach-agent $tcp
$ns at 1.0 "$ftp start"


# Printing the window size
proc plotWindow {tcpSource file} {
global ns
set time 0.1
set now [$ns now]
set cwnd [$tcpSource set cwnd_]
puts $file "$now $cwnd"
$ns at [expr $now+$time] "plotWindow $tcpSource $file" }
$ns at 1.1 "plotWindow $tcp $windowVsTime2"


# Telling nodes when the simulation ends
for {set i 0} {$i < $val(nn) } { incr i } {
    $ns at $val(stop) "$node_($i) reset";
```

```
}

$ns at $val(stop) "stop"
$ns at [expr $val(stop)+0.1]  "puts \"end simulation\" ; $ns halt"
proc stop {} {
    global ns tracefd
    $ns flush-trace
    close $tracefd
}

$ns run
```

8.6.3   SIMULATION RESULTS

Our simulation results for $n = 9, 20$ and 30 nodes are summarized in Tables 8.13-8.15, respectively.

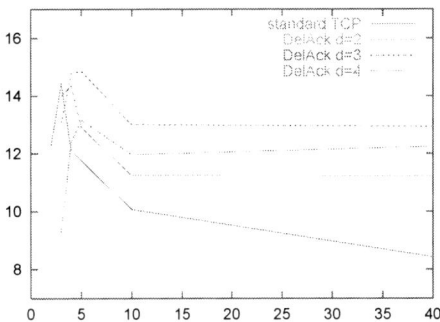

Figure 8.13: Throughput in pkt/sec for $n = 9$ as a function of the maximum window size.

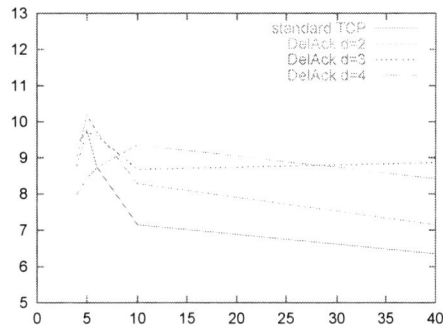

Figure 8.14: Throughput in pkt/sec for $n = 20$ as a function of the maximum window size.

We see that the standard Delayed Ack option ($d = 2$) slightly outperforms the standard TCP (yet with another value of maximum window size) for $n = 9$, and largely outperforms (more than 10%) the standard TCP for $n = 30$. A further improvement is obtained by the Delayed Ack with $d = 3$ (for both $n = 9$ as well as $n = 20$). But the most important improvement that we see is that all delayed ACK versions are better than the standard TCP for maximum window sizes of more than 10, with the options of $d = 3$ or $d = 4$ outperforming the standard delayed ACK option. For $n = 9$, the Delayed ACK version with $d = 3$ is seen to yield between 30% to 40% improvement over standard TCP for any maximum window sizes larger than 10; in that range it also outperforms standard TCP by 20%-30% for $n = 20$ and by $6\% - 20\%$ for $n = 30$. The version $d = 4$ performs

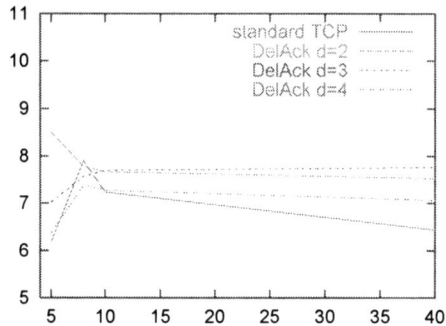

Figure 8.15: Throughput in pkt/sec for $n = 30$ as a function of the maximum window size.

even better for $n = 20$ for maximum windows between 10 to 25. An even better performance of delayed ACK can be obtained by optimizing over the timer duration of the Delayed Ack options, as we shall see later.

Yet the most important conclusion from the curves is the robustness of the Delayed Ack options. In practice, when we do not know the number of nodes, there is no reason to limit the maximum window size to a small value, since this could deteriorate the throughput considerably. When choosing large maximum window, the delayed ACK versions considerably outperform standard TCP. They achieve almost the optimal value that the standard TCP could achieve if it knew the number of nodes and could choose accordingly the maximum window.

For a fixed small size of maximum window size, the Delayed Ack option does not outperform the standard TCP version since most of the time, the window size limits the number of transmitted TCP packets to less than d, which means that the delayed ACK option has to wait until the timer (of 100ms by default) expires before generating an ACK; during that time the source cannot transmit packets.

Next, we plot the window size evolution for $n = 9$ for standard TCP and for TCP with delayed ACK option with $d = 3$. The window size is sampled every 0.1 sec. We see that although the maximum window size is 2000, the actual congestion window does not exceed the value of 13. We see from the figures that in standard TCP, losses are more frequent and more severe (resulting in timeouts) whereas the $d = 3$ version of delayed ACK does not give rise to timeouts.

In Figure 8.18 we present the evolution of the congestion window size for standard TCP with maximum window size of 3 for the case of 9 nodes. We know from [29] that a maximum size of between 2 and 3 should indeed give optimal performance (and this is confirmed in Figure 8.13). We see in Figure 8.18 that there are almost no losses. Note that the actual window size is the minimum between the congestion window (depicted in the Figure) and the maximum window size (whose value here is 3).

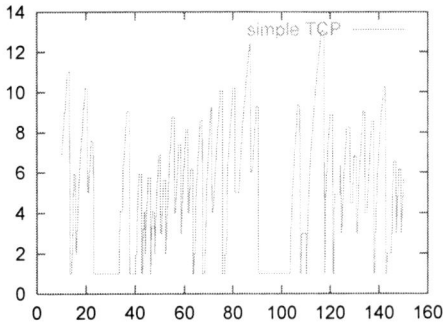

Figure 8.16: Window size evolution for standard TCP with maximum window of 2000.

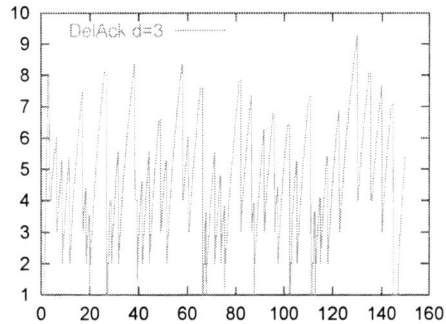

Figure 8.17: Window size evolution for DelAck TCP with $d = 3$, with maximum window of 2000.

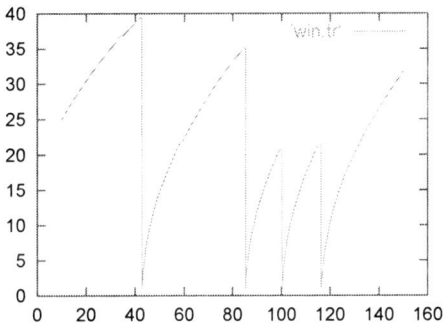

Figure 8.18: Window size evolution for standard TCP (delayed ACK disabled) with 9 nodes and maximum window size of 3.

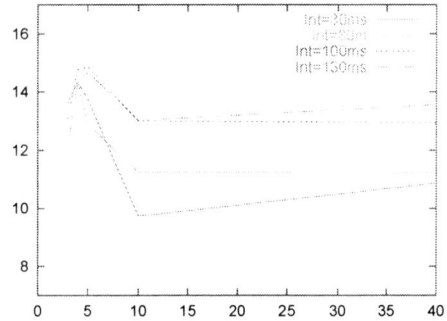

Figure 8.19: The influence of Delayed Ack interval on TCP throughput, as a function of the maximum window size. $d = 3$.

In the previous Figures, all versions using delayed Acks had the default interval of 100msec (as explained in the Introduction). Next, we vary the interval length and check its impact on throughput, see Figure 8.19. We consider the delayed ACK version with $d = 3$. We see that the default value performs quite well, although for small maximum windows, shorter intervals perform slightly better, whereas with large maximum window, a larger interval (130ms) is slightly better. We tried to further increase the time interval beyond 130ms but then the throughput decreased.

Finally, we consider the case of $n = 3$ nodes. In that case the hidden terminal phenomenon does not occur anymore, so we do not observe TCP losses for any value of window size. Even then, delayed ACKs can be used to improve considerably the performance. This is illustrated in Table 8.1 that gives the number of TCP packets successfully received within 149 sec for $n = 3$. Since there are no losses, then as long as d is greater than the max window, we expect to improve the performance

WinMax	Standard TCP	Delayed Ack Versions		
	Standard	$d = 2$	$d = 3$	$d = 4$
3	6068	6602	6763	2699
2000	6094	6565	6779	6888

Table 8.1: Number of transmitter packets during 149sec for $n = 3$ as a function of the maximum window size.

as d gets larger, since TCP packets compete with less ACKs. This is indeed confirmed in Table 8.1. The improvement that increases from 10% to 15% as d grows from 2 to 4, does not depend on the maximum window (as long as it is greater than d). However for $d = 4$ we see, as can be expected, that we get a bad performance for a maximum window of 3, since the destination always needs to wait till the 100ms interval of the Delayed Ack option expires in order to send an ACK (since the windows allows for sending only 3 data packets).

8.7   EXERCISES

8.1. We have restricted the study in this chapter to a permanent TCP connection. Repeat the experience with short TCP connections. Check the case where TCP is used by an FTP and then consider HTTP type traffic (using TCP). What conclusions can we draw?

8.2. Repeat the simulations on TCP over ad-hoc networks with a star topology instead of a linear one. What are the conclusions?

CHAPTER 9

Classical queueing models

NS-2 simulator can be used to simulate classical queueing models. In the simplest classical models, the time between packets arrival is random and has some general probability distribution, and the time it takes to transmit a packet is random as well distributed according to some other distribution. The fact that the transmission time varies may reflect a situation of a constant transmission rate but a varying size of a packet. The mathematical analysis of queueing example we present here as well as many others can be found in the excellent book by Kleinrock [39] on queueing theory.

9.1 SIMULATING AN M/M/1, M/D/1 AND D/M/1 QUEUES

The queueing example which is the simplest for mathematical analysis is the $M/M/1$ queue: inter-arrival times are exponentially distributed with some parameter, say λ, and the transmission duration of a packet has an exponential distribution with another parameter, say μ. One packet can be transmitted at a time, and the buffer size is infinite. If we denote $\rho = \lambda/\mu$, the time average number of packets in the system is given by

$$E[Q] = \frac{\rho}{1 - \rho}. \tag{9.1}$$

In Listing 9.1 we present a simulation of this queue. The simulation produces a trace file out.tr with all events, and also a monitor-queue trace called qm.out, as discussed in Section 4.3. By plotting columns 5 (queue size in packets) against column 1 (time) we obtain (see Figure 9.1) the queue length evolution. The average simulated queue size over 1000sec is 9.69117, a good approximation of the value 10 obtained by (9.1).

Note that we use a simpler way to declare and manipulate random variables than the one described in Section 2.7: we do not declare generators and seeds.

It is quite interesting to analyze the simulation results and try to find the possible reasons for the difference. Once we do so we may find several reasons for the simulation's imprecisions (and use the conclusions to improve the simulations):

Listing 9.1: Tcl script mm1.tcl for simulating an M/M/1 queue.

```
set ns [new Simulator]

set tf [open out.tr w]
$ns trace-all $tf
```

```
set lambda 30.0
set mu      33.0

set n1 [$ns node]
set n2 [$ns node]
# Since packet sizes will be rounded to an integer
# number of bytes, we should have large packets and
# to have small rounding errors, and so we take large bandwidth
set link [$ns simplex-link $n1 $n2 100kb 0ms DropTail]
$ns queue-limit $n1 $n2 100000

# generate random interarrival times and packet sizes
set InterArrivalTime [new RandomVariable/Exponential]
$InterArrivalTime set avg_ [expr 1/$lambda]
set pktSize [new RandomVariable/Exponential]
$pktSize set avg_ [expr 100000.0/(8*$mu)]

set src [new Agent/UDP]
$ns attach-agent $n1 $src

# queue monitoring
set qmon [$ns monitor-queue $n1 $n2 [open qm.out w] 0.1]
$link queue-sample-timeout

proc finish {} {
    global ns tf
    $ns flush-trace
    close $tf
    exit 0
}

proc sendpacket {} {
    global ns src InterArrivalTime pktSize
    set time [$ns now]
    $ns at [expr $time + [$InterArrivalTime value]] "sendpacket"
    set bytes [expr round ([$pktSize value])]
    $src send $bytes
}

set sink [new Agent/Null]
$ns attach-agent $n2 $sink
```

```
$ns connect $src $sink
$ns at 0.0001 "sendpacket"
$ns at 1000.0 "finish"

$ns run
```

- The formula (9.1) counts the whole packet that is being transmitted, whereas the simulation counts only the fraction of the transmitted packet that is still in the queue. This difference should make the simulated result lower than the exact one by about 0.5 per packet.

- On the other hand, the simulated packets turn out to be truncated at the value of 1kbyte, which is the default size of a UDP packet. Thus transmission times are a little shorter than we intended them to be. To correct this, one should change the default maximum packet size, for example to 100000. This is done by adding the line

```
$src set packetSize_ 100000
```

  after the command `set src [new Agent/UDP]`.

- The simulation time is not sufficiently long. With a duration of 20000, we get a much more precise value.

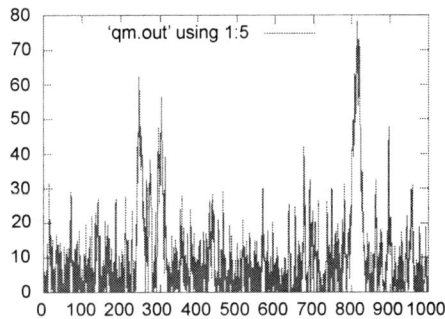

Figure 9.1: Evolution of an M/M/1 queue size.

The M/D/1 queue is one where inter-arrival times are exponentially distributed but transmission times of packets are constant. To simulate it, simply replace the random variable pktSize by its average. Similarly, a D/M/1 queue is one where transmission duration has an exponential distribution and inter-arrival times are constant. To simulate this, we should replace the InterarrivalTime random variable by its average.

9.2   FINITE QUEUE

In the above simulation, we used very large buffers to avoid losses. One can use smaller buffers and observe losses. For M/M/1/K queue with K buffers, the loss probability is given by

$$P(loss) = \frac{\rho^K}{\sum_{i=0}^{K} \rho^i}.$$

The way to compute the loss probability from the simulation is simply to divide the total number of losses by the total number of arrivals, both given in the last line of the monitor-queue file.

Listing 9.2: Tcl script mm1k.tcl for simulating an MM1 queue.

```
set ns [new Simulator]

set tf [open out.tr w]
$ns trace-all $tf

set lambda    30.0
set mu        33.0
set qsize     2
set duration  2000

set n1 [$ns node]
set n2 [$ns node]
set link [$ns simplex-link $n1 $n2 100kb 0ms DropTail]
$ns queue-limit $n1 $n2 $qsize

# generate random interarrival times and packet sizes
set InterArrivalTime [new RandomVariable/Exponential]
$InterArrivalTime set avg_ [expr 1/$lambda]
set pktSize [new RandomVariable/Exponential]
$pktSize set avg_ [expr 100000.0/(8*$mu)]

set src [new Agent/UDP]
$src set packetSize_ 100000
$ns attach-agent $n1 $src

# queue monitoring
set qmon [$ns monitor-queue $n1 $n2 [open qm.out w] 0.1]
$link queue-sample-timeout

proc finish {} {
```

```
    global ns tf
    $ns flush-trace
    close $tf
    exit 0
}


proc sendpacket {} {
    global ns src InterArrivalTime pktSize
    set time [$ns now]
    $ns at [expr $time + [$InterArrivalTime value]] "sendpacket"
    set bytes [expr round ([$pktSize value])]
    $src send $bytes
}


set sink [new Agent/Null]
$ns attach-agent $n2 $sink
$ns connect $src $sink
$ns at 0.0001 "sendpacket"
$ns at $duration "finish"


$ns run
```

Adding the command $src set packetSize_ 100000 as mentioned in the previous Section, we get very good agreement between the simulation and the formula. For example, for $K = 2$ we get $P(loss) = 0.298$ by simulation of duration of 2000sec and $P(loss) = 0.3025$ through the above formula. For $K = 5$ we obtain 0.131 and 0.128 by simulation and through the formula, respectively. The script is given in Table 9.2.

Remark: For $K = 1$, the simulation does not work well; in that case all arriving packets are lost!

9.3 EXERCISES

9.1. Write a tcl script for simulating an infinite server queue with a Poisson arrival process of packets, where the service time of packets are i.i.d. with a general distribution (this queue is known as an M/G/∞ queue). In this system there are no waiting times: each arriving packet is served by another server immediately upon arrival. Thus if packet i requires B_i service time and it arrives at time T_i then it leaves the system at time $T_i + B_i$.

9.2. Assume that 10 sources, which send files of data to a common destination using TCP, share a common bottleneck link. The sequence of times at which source i starts to send the ith file is a Poisson process, which is independent of arrivals from other sources. All connections are assumed to have the same propagation delay. There has been a rich amount of research that used queueing models to compute the expected time needed to transmit a file. Several have proposed the processor sharing queueing discipline to model the behavior of the system at a connection level. This exercise proposes to check this statement for the case of exponentially distributed file sizes. To do so, find out what is a processor sharing queue. Explain how the parameter of the model are computed (as a function of the parameters of the TCP connections). Simulate both, the initial scenario of TCP connections that share a bottleneck link, as well as an abstract queueing model using the processor sharing discipline. Compare the results and check for what parameters the processor sharing queue is a good approximation for the session level behavior.

9.3.   Next use the M/G/∞ queue instead of the processor sharing queue and check for what parameters it provides for more accurate modeling of the original problem than the processor sharing queue.

C H A P T E R   10

Tcl and C++ linkage

This last chapter is more advanced than previous ones and we usually do not include it in courses for beginners. We chose to include it in this book in order to ease the access to those beginners who might be confronted with the need to perform more advanced tasks.

To be more specific, NS-2 is composed of two object oriented languages: C++ and Otcl. If one wants to create new modules or to change the current ones, one has to have at least basic programming notions in C++, or more generally, in object oriented programming. Without such background the reader has little chance to follow this Chapter.

There is a hierarchy of classes in C++ and also in Otcl. The exact place of each group of classes in the NS-2 directory will depend on the version of the NS-2 simulator that one uses.

For example, in the "common" directory there are all the classes that are common to all simulations, like the scheduler, the agent, the packet, etc. We recommend to spend time at the beginning exploring the hierarchy of NS-2. But if one creates a class (or many classes) on the C++ hierarchy, how can we use them from the tcl script? The C++ classes that we want to access from the tcl script have to be bound to classes in the Otcl hierarchy.

For binding two classes (a C++ class with an Otcl class) we have to follow some steps:

At first one has to create the C++ class. The place where one will put the files will depend on the functionality of this class. For example, if we code a new version of the TCP protocol, we shall put the *tcp-mine.h* and *tcp-mine.cc* files under the tcp directory.

In general, we do not create a class from scratch, but we let it inherit from a more general class in the NS-2 C++ hierarchy. If we want to develop a new Application, we will let our class inherit from the Application class (in the app directory).

In the example that we shall use we want to create a new traffic generator. We wish it to inherit from the abstract class TrafficGenerator. The TrafficGenerator class has some methods that we will re-define; there are the virtual methods.

```
class normalTraffic : public TrafficGenerator {
 public:
        normalTraffic();
        virtual void timeout();
        virtual double next_interval(int&);
        int command(int argc, const char*const* argv);
 protected:
        void init();
```

```
        double avg_;
        double std_;
        double off_;
        double rate_;      /* send rate during on time (bps) */
        double interval_; /* packet inter-arrival
time during burst (sec) */
        unsigned int rem_; /* number of packets left in current burst */

        NormalRandomVariable burstlen;
        ExponentialRandomVariable offtime;
};
```

Our class is called normalTraffic. We now have to bind it with the correspondent Otcl class. The first thing to do is to choose a name for the Otcl class; we don't need to call them in the same way, but is the common way to do.

```
static class normalTrafficClass : public TclClass {
 public:
        normalTrafficClass() : TclClass("Application/Traffic/Normal") {}
        TclObject* create(int, const char*const*) {
                return (new normalTraffic());
        }
} class_normaltraffic;
```

In these lines we said that we will create a static class which inherits from the TclClass. In the first line after public we establish how our class will be called from the tcl script. In our example one will have to use: set traf [new Application/Traffic/Normal] in order to create an object of this class. We said in the return clause the C++ class that we will use when instantiating this Otcl class. Remark that we have to give a name also at the end.

In the constructor of the C++ class we have to bind the variables that we shall use and whose values are given in the tcl script (or in the defaults file).

```
normalTraffic::normalTraffic()
{
        bind_bw("rate_", &rate_);
        bind("avg_", &avg_);
        bind("off_", &off_);
        bind("std_", &std_);
        bind("packetSize_", &size_);
}
```

We use the same name for most of them, but we can use a different name for the tcl (like packetSize_) and another for the C++ (like size_); the way of calling the attributes is up to the programmer, but it is a good practice to use the same way of that of the main classes of NS-2.

Once we have complete the program, we have to update two files: the ns-defaults.tcl in the tcl/lib directory, where we write the default values for the variables we have made a bind in our class and the Makefile, where we said to compile also our new class. After that we have to compile, using the make command and then we can test using a tcl script which uses the recently created class.

In the following example we have created a new traffic generator, which is an on off source, that in the on periods generates packets following a Normal distribution.

Listing 10.1: C++ script Normal Traffic Generator.

```
/*
 * Normal Traffic Generator
 */

#include "trafgen.h"
#include "ranvar.h"

class normalTraffic : public TrafficGenerator {
 public:
        normalTraffic();
        virtual void timeout();
        virtual double next_interval(int&);
        int command(int argc, const char*const* argv);
 protected:
        void init();
        double avg_;    /* average of the normal dist. */
        double std_;    /* standard deviation */
        double off_;    /* average off time */
        double rate_;     /* send rate during on time (bps) */
        double interval_; /* packet inter-arrival
time during burst (sec) */
        unsigned int rem_; /* number of packets left in current burst */

        NormalRandomVariable burstlen;
        ExponentialRandomVariable offtime;
};

static class normalTrafficClass : public TclClass {
 public:
        normalTrafficClass() : TclClass("Application/Traffic/Normal") {}
        TclObject* create(int, const char*const*) {
                return (new normalTraffic());
        }
```

```
} class_normaltraffic;

int normalTraffic::command(int argc, const char*const* argv){
        if(argc==3){
                if (strcmp(argv[1], "use-rng") == 0){
                        burstlen.seed((char *)argv[2]);
                        offtime.seed((char *)argv[2]);
                        return (TCL_OK);
                }
        }
        return Application::command(argc,argv);
}

normalTraffic::normalTraffic()
{
        bind_bw("rate_", &rate_);
        bind("avg_", &avg_);
        bind("off_", &off_);
        bind("std_", &std_);
        bind("packetSize_", &size_);
}

void normalTraffic::init()
{
        if (agent_)
                agent_->set_pkttype(PT_EXP);
        interval_ = (double)(size_ << 3)/(double)rate_;
        burstlen.setavg(avg_);
        burstlen.setstd(std_);
        offtime.setavg(off_);
        rem_=0;
}

double normalTraffic::next_interval(int& size)
{
   double t = interval_;

        if (rem_ == 0) {
                /* compute number of packets in next burst */
                rem_ = int(burstlen.value() +.5);
                /* make sure we got at least 1 */
                if (rem_ == 0)
```

```
                        rem_  =  1;
            /* start of an idle period, compute idle time */
            t += offtime.value();
      }
      rem_--;

      size = size_;
      return(t);
}


void normalTraffic::timeout()
{
      if (! running_)
            return;
      agent_->sendmsg(size_);
      nextPkttime_ = next_interval(size_);
      timer_.resched(nextPkttime_);
}
```

The method command allows us to check if there are parameters passed to the class. In this case we check if one wants to use a different random number generator than the default one. If it is the case, we pass it to our two Random Variables (RVs).

In the init method we initialize the RVs and the interval between packets, using the values of the bound variables. The next interval gives to the Traffic Generator the next step for sending data, which is the next packet if there is data to send, or the wake up time after the off period.

The timeout method is the same as in the Traffic Generator, but if we like to change it then it is better to reload it on the new class. This is the method that actually calls the agent for sending the packet and then schedule the next event (at the time to send the next packet) on the scheduler.

In the next listing 10.2 we show how to use this newly created class.

Listing 10.2: Tcl script rdrop.tcl for testing the new class.

```
set ns [new Simulator]

proc finish {} {
        exit 0
}

set n0 [$ns node]
set n1 [$ns node]

$ns duplex-link $n0 $n1 1Mb 10ms DropTail
```

```
set Udp [new Agent/UDP]
$ns attach-agent $n0 $Udp

set null [new Agent/Null]
$ns attach-agent $n1 $null

$ns connect $Udp $null

set traf [new Application/Traffic/Normal]
$traf set packetSize_ 1500
$traf set off_ 10ms
$traf set avg_ 5
$traf set std_ 5
$traf set rate_ 1Mb

$traf attach-agent $Udp

$ns at 0.1 "$traf start"
$ns at 5.0 "$traf stop"

$ns at 5.1 "finish"

$ns run
```

We call the creation of the class with the name we use on the NormalTrafficClass method. Then we give values to the parameters (if we omit some of them, they will take the default values). The avg_ is the average number of packets to be send during the on period, and std_ is the standard deviation; those are the parameters of the normal distribution.

This is a very simple example of how to create new classes within the NS-2 hierarchy. Of course, if one wants to create a new module, for example to simulate a new protocol, then many C++ classes have to be created, some of them will be linked with the Otcl hierarchy and others not. It depends in the design of the new modules and the interface one wants to have with the final user.

APPENDIX A

Appendix I: Random variables: background

Random variables with different distributions can be created in ns. Due to its important role in traffic modeling and in network simulation, we briefly recall the definitions and moments of main random variables in Appendix A. For more background, one can consult, e.g., http://www.xycoon.com/.

For a random variable (RV) X, we denote $F_x(s) = P(X \leq s)$, $\overline{F}_x(s) = P(X > s)$ and by $f_x(s)$ we denote its density. (We often omit the subscript x.)

1. **Pareto distribution.** A Pareto RV is defined through

$$\overline{F}(s) = (k/s)^{\beta},$$

where k is the minimum size and $\beta > 0$ is the so called "shape parameter". It is defined on the range $X \geq k$. The density is given by

$$f(s) = \frac{\beta k^{\beta}}{s^{\beta+1}}.$$

The expectation and other moments are

$$
\begin{aligned}
E[X] &= \frac{\beta k}{\beta - 1}, & 1 < \beta \\
E[X^n] &= \frac{\beta k^n}{\beta - n}, & n < \beta
\end{aligned}
$$

The nth moment is infinite if $n \geq \beta$.

The size of files transferred over the Internet is often characterized with a Pareto distribution with $1 < \beta \leq 2$, see [20, 54]. A typical value is $\beta = 1.2$ [14]. A typical value for the expected size of a file in Internet transfers is 10Kbits. In the context of WEB transfers, typical values are $\beta = 1.1$ and $k = 81.5$Kbytes (see [23, p.34-35]).

2. **The exponential Random Variable.** An exponentially distributed RV with parameter α is defined through

$$\overline{F}(s) = \exp(-\alpha s), \quad f(s) = \alpha \exp(-\alpha s).$$

All its moments exist and are given by

$$E[X^n] = \frac{n!}{\alpha^n}.$$

In a WEB transfer, Pareto distributed transfers are typically separated with exponentially distributed silence times ("thinking times") with average duration of $\alpha^{-1} = 5sec$ [21].

3. **Normal distribution.** It is characterized by two parameters (μ, σ^2). Its probability density is given by

$$f(s) = \frac{1}{2\pi} \exp\left[-\frac{1}{2}\left(\frac{s - \mu}{\sigma}\right)^2\right]$$

and its first moments by

$$E[X] = \mu, \quad E[X^2] = \mu^2 + \sigma^2.$$

This distribution is mostly used to describe thermal noise that should be taken into account when computing the signal to noise ratio in radio links.

4. **Lognormal distribution.** It is characterized by two parameters (μ, σ^2). Its density function is given by

$$f(s) = \frac{\exp\left[-\frac{1}{2}\left(\frac{ln(s) - \mu}{\sigma}\right)^2\right]}{\sqrt{2\pi\sigma^2 s^2}}.$$

and its moments are given by

$$E[X^n] = \exp\left[j\mu + \frac{1}{2}(j\sigma)^2\right].$$

X is lognormally distributed with parameters (μ, σ^2) if and only if $\ln(X)$ is normally distributed with the same parameters. It can thus be written as $X = \exp(Y)$ where $Y \sim N(\mu, \sigma^2)$. In CDMA wireless communications, the received power from power controlled sources with fading channels have lognormal distribution where σ is typically between 0.3 and 3dB [6].

5. **Gamma distribution** A Gamma distributed RV with parameters (α, r) has a probability density of

$$f(s) = \frac{\alpha^r}{\Gamma[r]} s^{r-1} e^{-\alpha r}$$

where Γ is the Γ-function which satisfies $\Gamma(r) = (r - 1)!$ for r integers. The moments are

$$E[X] = \frac{r}{\alpha}, \quad E[X^n] = \alpha^{-n} \prod_{i=0}^{n-1} (r + i), n > 1.$$

The distribution is defined on the range $0 \leq s \leq \infty$, and its parameters are defined for $\alpha > 0$ and $r > 0$. In the special case where r is an integer, this distribution is called the Erlang distribution.

APPENDIX B

Appendix II: Confidence intervals

In this Appendix we briefly recall the notion of confidence intervals that addresses the question of how to estimate the correctness of a simulated result.

A standard way to obtain a better precision of performance measures obtained from simulations is to take the average of several "independent" runs (independence can be obtained by using different seeds and generators). Indeed, by the strong law of large numbers, the average $\overline{X}$ of n independent and identically distributed values $X_i, i = 1, ..., n$ approaches the expectation $E[X]$ which we may wish to estimate.

Our goal is to check how accurate $\overline{X}$ is as an estimator of $E[X]$. In particular, we wish to determine some constant d such that the probability that $\overline{X} \in \left[E[X] - d, E[X] + d \right]$ be at least $1-\alpha$, where α is some small error probability (say 5%).

The variance of $\overline{X}$ is given by

$$Var(\overline{X}) = \frac{\sigma^2}{n}$$

Let σ^2 be the variance of X_i. If we knew σ, we could estimate the accuracy of $\overline{X}$ as a prediction of $E[X]$ by using the central limit theorem, which implies that

$$\sqrt{n}\frac{\overline{X} - E[X]}{\sigma} \sim N(0, 1).$$

If $\Psi(x)$ is the probability that a standard Gaussian RV is not greater than x, then this suggests that

$$P\left(\overline{X} \in \left[E[X] - d, E[X] + d \right]\right) = \Psi\left(\frac{d\sqrt{n}}{\sigma}\right) - \Psi\left(-\frac{d\sqrt{n}}{\sigma}\right). \tag{B.1}$$

For example, if $\alpha = 5\%$ then the constant d that guarantees that $P\left(\overline{X} \in \left[E[X] - d, E[X] + d \right]\right) \geq 1 - \alpha = 0.95$ is given by $d = 1.96\sigma/\sqrt{n}$.

In practice, σ is typically unknown and has to be estimated together with $E[X]$. One could use $\sum_{i=1}^{n}(X_i - \overline{X}_i)^2/n$ as an estimator for σ^2, but this would give a biased estimator, i.e., an estimator whose expected value differs from σ^2. Instead, the estimator

$$S^2 = \frac{\sum_{i=1}^{n}(X_i - \overline{X}_i)^2}{n-1}$$

turns out to be unbiased, i.e., $E[S^2] = \sigma^2$, see [50, p. 111]. It is called the *sample variance*.

One then uses (B.1) with S replacing σ as an approximation of the probability that $\overline{X}$ is within the confidence interval.

The next script in awk can be used to compute the sample average of an output file, where we average over the numbers appearing in the 3rd column:

```
BEGIN { FS = "\t"} { nl++ } { s = s + $3 } END {print "del : " s/nl}
```

If this script is written in a file called "thpR.awk" and the values of X_i's are given in the third column of a file called "a40n" then one should type

```
awk -f thpR.awk a40n
```

in order to get $\overline{X}$.

The following then computes the confidence interval related to $\alpha = 5\%$:

```
BEGIN { FS = "\t"} {ln++}{ d = $3 - t } { s2 = s2 + d*d } END \
{s=sqrt(s2/(ln-1)); print "sample variance: " s " \
Conf. Int. 95%: " t "+/-" 1.96*s/sqrt(ln)}
```

If "ConfInt.awk" is the name of the file containig this script, type

```
awk -v t=XXX -f ConfInt.awk a40n
```

where instead of XXX one should put the value of $\overline{X}$. This will give both the sample variance as well as the required confidence interval.

APPENDIX C

Appendix III: A small overview on NS-3

In this Appendix we briefly show some simple examples for NS-3.

In NS-3 you can take a look to the file `samples/main-attribute-value.cc` to learn how to set the default values for the attributes you need to specify. See also `http://www.nsnam.org/docs/manual/html/attributes.html` for learning how to deal with attributes in NS-3.

C.1   INITIALIZATION AND TERMINATION IN NS-3

In NS-3 we can stop the simulation using the "Stop" method `Simulator::Stop (Seconds (10.0));` of the simulator which can have "Time" as parameter. If this method is called with a parameter, the simulation will end when all the events with timestamps less than the stop time passed as parameter have been processed. If no parameter is passed to this method, the simulation will stop after processing the event which called the Stop method.

In NS-3 the simulation begins using the command `Simulator::Run ();`. This command will run the simulation until one of the following conditions hold : "

- no events are present anymore

- the user called Simulator::stop

- the user called Simulator::stopAtUs and the expiration time of the next event to be processed is greater than or equal to the stop time [2]."

The method "Destroy" `Simulator::Destroy ();` is called at the end of the simulation in order to free the memory allocated by the Simulator.

C.2   DEFINITION OF A NETWORK TOPOLOGY IN NS-3

In order to create two nodes with a point-to-point link between them we use the following code:

```
NodeContainer nodes;
nodes.Create (2);

PointToPointHelper pointToPoint;
pointToPoint.SetDeviceAttribute ("DataRate", StringValue ("5Mbps"));
pointToPoint.SetChannelAttribute ("Delay", StringValue ("2ms"));

NetDeviceContainer p2pDevices;
p2pDevices = pointToPoint.Install (nodes);
```

The two first lines are used to create a container for the nodes, and to create two of them. Next, we use the class "PointToPointHelper" which will be used for installing the devices into the nodes with the corresponding channel attributes: 5Mbps of data rate and 2ms of delay. By default it creates a DropTail queue with a maximum capacity of 100 packets.

C.3 TRANSPORT PROTOCOLS AND APPLICATIONS IN NS-3

In NS-3 there is no Agent class for specifying the transport protocol, but a module called "InternetStack" which provides the necessary classes for the TCP/IP(v4 and v6)-related components.

```
InternetStackHelper stack;
stack.Install (nodes);

Ipv4AddressHelper address;
address.SetBase ("10.1.1.0", "255.255.255.0");
Ipv4InterfaceContainer interfaces = address.Assign (p2pDevices);
uint16_t port = 9;  // the echo port number
UdpEchoServerHelper server (port);
ApplicationContainer apps = server.Install (nodes.Get(1));
apps.Start (Seconds (1.0));
apps.Stop (Seconds (10.0));

uint32_t packetSize = 1024;
uint32_t maxPacketCount = 5;
Time interPacketInterval = Seconds (1.5);
UdpEchoClientHelper client (i.GetAddress (1), port);
client.SetAttribute ("MaxPackets", UintegerValue (maxPacketCount));
client.SetAttribute ("Interval", TimeValue (interPacketInterval));
client.SetAttribute ("PacketSize", UintegerValue (packetSize));
apps = client.Install (nodes.Get (0));
apps.Start (Seconds (2.0));
apps.Stop (Seconds (10.0));
```

We use the class "InternetStackHelper" in order to install the internet stack. We declare the IP address to use. The interfaces of the nodes will have then IP addresses: 10.1.1.1 and 10.1.1.2.

All the implemented classes of applications in NS-3 are derived from the "Application" class. There are a BulkSendApplication, OnOffApplication, PacketSink, Ping6, Radvd, UdpClientServer, and UdpEcho applications.

In the script above we use the application UdpEcho, with its helper classes "EdpEchoServer-Helper" and "UdpEchoClientHelper". Once the application is declared, we install it in a node (node 0 for the client and 1 for the server) and we declare the beginning and end time for each application.

C.4   SCHEDULING EVENTS IN NS-3

NS-3 is also a discrete event simulator. The class "Scheduler" maintains the event list. There are five different schedulers in NS-3 at the moment: CalendarScheduler, HeapScheduler, ListScheduler, MapScheduler and Ns2CalendarScheduler.

By default the MapScheduler is used, but you can change the sched-uler, as well as all the Global Values, by the command line, for example: `./waf --run "<your_program_name> --SchedulerType=ns3::HeapScheduler"` will run the simulation with the HeapScheduler.

C.5   TRACING IN NS-3

NS-3 has a Tracing API that is well documented in the manual [3]. Here we will show only the base tracing using the Trace Helpers.

```
AsciiTraceHelper ascii;
helper.EnableAsciiAll (ascii.CreateFileStream ("trace.tr"));
helper.EnablePcapAll ("trace", true);
```

In NS-3 we can declare the tracefiles anywhere in the main file.

In order to create trace files you can insert these three lines of code into your program. The helper object depends on your topology, for example you have to use a CsmaHelper if you want to trace the packets in a csma channel. After running the simulation you will obtain a file trace.tr with the trace in ascii. The last line will create some ".pcap" files where the trace prefix are the nodes. For example, if there is traffic between node 1 and node 2 you will have a file trace-1-2.pcap. These pcap files can be read with tcpdump or wireshark.

C.6   CREATING RANDOM VARIABLES IN NS-3

NS-3 uses the same implementation of Random Variables as NS-2.

Listing C.1 does the same as the example we saw with NS-2. By default the global seed for all rng streams is set to 1 and the run number is also set to 1. One can see these global values using: `./waf --run "scratch/<your_program_name> --PrintGlobals"`

Listing C.1: C++ program for Random Variables test in ns-3.

```cpp
#include <iostream>
#include "ns3/random-variable.h"

using namespace ns3;
using namespace std;

int main(int argc, char *argv[])
{
// These two lines are not needed, the values are the same by default,
// only here to show how to change the
Seed and Run number into the program.
SeedManager::SetSeed(1);
SeedManager::SetRun (1);

ExponentialVariable r0(5.0);
r0.GetValue () ;
UniformVariable r1(0.0, 10.0);
ExponentialVariable r2(5.0);
NormalVariable r3(1.0, 16.0);
ParetoVariable r4(1.0, 1.5);
cout << "Uniform \t Exponential \t Normal \t Pareto" <<endl;
for(int i = 0; i<10; i++)
    cout << r1.GetValue () << "\t" << r2.GetValue () << "\t"
        << r3.GetValue () << "\t" << r4.GetValue () << endl;
}
```

The Seed and the Run number can be changed by using the command line:

`./waf --run "scratch/udp-echo --RngRun=4"`

In Listing C.1 we declare an Exponential Variable with average 5.0, then a Uniform Variable (r1) between 0 and 10, another Exponential Variable (r2), a Normal Variable (r3) with average 1.0 and variance 16.0[1], and a Pareto Variable (r4) with average 1.0 and shape 1.5. Then we print each of these values. In NS-3 each new Random Variable created will use a new substream.

C.7   SHORT OVERVIEW OF TCP IN NS-3

In the following example we create three nodes, which are connected by two different point to point networks. The node in the middle has two devices in order to send packets from a network to the other. Most parts of Listing C.2 have been explained in previous sections. We will explain here only

---

[1]In NS-2 the normal variable has as parameters the average and the standard deviation.

how to trace the value of the cwnd. We create a method called CwndTracer which will write on a file the time and the value of cwnd at this time. This method will be invoked by the callback each time the congestion window of the Tcp socket on node zero will change. It is declared in the following way:

```
Config::ConnectWithoutContext,"/NodeList/0/$ns3::TcpL4Protocol/
          SocketList/0/CongestionWindow", MakeCallback (&CwndTracer));
```

This has to be scheduled after the Application starts. We can choose the version of TCP we will use with the line:

```
Config::SetDefault ("ns3::TcpL4Protocol::SocketType", TypeIdValue(TypeId::
          LookupByName ("ns3::TcpTahoe")));
```

For more information, refer to the NS-3 manual [3].

Listing C.2: A TCP example on NS-3.

```cpp
#include <iostream>
#include <fstream>
#include "ns3/simulator-module.h"
#include "ns3/node-module.h"
#include "ns3/core-module.h"
#include "ns3/helper-module.h"
#include "ns3/global-route-manager.h"
#include "ns3/ipv4-global-routing-helper.h"


using namespace ns3;


NS_LOG_COMPONENT_DEFINE ("simpleTCP");


//global variables
static std::ofstream window;


static void
CwndTracer (uint32_t oldval, uint32_t newval)
{
  window << ns3::Simulator::Now().GetSeconds() <<" "<< newval/1024 <<std::endl;
}


int main (int argc, char *argv[])
{
  LogComponentEnable ("simpleTCP", LOG_LEVEL_ALL);

  // Set up some default values for the simulation.
```

```
Config::SetDefault ("ns3::OnOffApplication::PacketSize", UintegerValue (1024));
Config::SetDefault ("ns3::OnOffApplication::DataRate", DataRateValue (2000000));
Config::SetDefault ("ns3::DropTailQueue::MaxPackets", UintegerValue(uint32_t(20)));

CommandLine cmd;
cmd.Parse (argc, argv);
window.open("window.tr");

NS_LOG_INFO ("Creating␣nodes..");
// We create three nodes
Ptr<Node> n0 = CreateObject<Node> ();
Ptr<Node> n1 = CreateObject<Node> ();
Ptr<Node> n2 = CreateObject<Node> ();

NS_LOG_INFO ("Creating␣Topology..");
NodeContainer n0n1;
NodeContainer n1n2;
n0n1.Add(n0);
n0n1.Add(n1);
n1n2.Add(n1);
n1n2.Add(n2);

// Container for all nodes
NodeContainer contAllNodes;
contAllNodes.Add(n0);
contAllNodes.Add(n1);
contAllNodes.Add(n2);

// Point2point network 1
PointToPointHelper p2pNet1;
p2pNet1.SetDeviceAttribute ("DataRate", DataRateValue (2000000));
p2pNet1.SetChannelAttribute ("Delay", TimeValue (MilliSeconds (5)));

// Point2point network 2
PointToPointHelper p2pNet2;
p2pNet2.SetDeviceAttribute ("DataRate", DataRateValue (1000000));
p2pNet2.SetChannelAttribute ("Delay", TimeValue (MilliSeconds (5)));

// NetDeviceContainers
NetDeviceContainer dev1 = p2pNet1.Install(n0n1);
NetDeviceContainer dev2 = p2pNet2.Install(n1n2);
```

```
// Install Internet stack in all nodes
InternetStackHelper stack;
stack.Install (contAllNodes);

NS_LOG_INFO ("Add IP addresses..");
Ipv4AddressHelper ipv4;

// First Network
ipv4.SetBase ("194.57.1.0", "255.255.255.0");
Ipv4InterfaceContainer ipIfaceN0N1 = ipv4.Assign (dev1);

// Second Network
ipv4.SetBase ("194.57.2.0", "255.255.255.0");
Ipv4InterfaceContainer ipIfaceN1N2 = ipv4.Assign (dev2);
Ipv4GlobalRoutingHelper::PopulateRoutingTables ();

// Create TCP Sink
uint16_t port = 10600;
Address SinkLocalAddress(InetSocketAddress (Ipv4Address::GetAny (), port));
PacketSinkHelper sinkHelper ("ns3::TcpSocketFactory",SinkLocalAddress);
ApplicationContainer sinkApp = sinkHelper.Install (n1n2.Get (1));
sinkApp.Start (Seconds (0.0));
sinkApp.Stop (Seconds (1000.0));

// Create Application for generating packets
OnOffHelper clientHelper ("ns3::TcpSocketFactory", Address ());
clientHelper.SetAttribute ("OnTime", RandomVariableValue(ConstantVariable (1)));
clientHelper.SetAttribute ("OffTime", RandomVariableValue(ConstantVariable (0)));
ApplicationContainer clientApps;
AddressValue remoteAddress (InetSocketAddress (ipIfaceN1N2.GetAddress (1),
                                                          port));
clientHelper.SetAttribute ("Remote", remoteAddress);
clientApps.Add(clientHelper.Install (nOn1.Get(0)));

clientApps.Start (Seconds (1.0));
clientApps.Stop (Seconds (300.0));

// Set default Socket type to one of the Tcp Sockets
Config::SetDefault ("ns3::TcpL4Protocol::SocketType",
                    TypeIdValue(TypeId::LookupByName ("ns3::TcpTahoe" )));

Simulator::Schedule (Seconds (1.1),
```

```
  Config::ConnectWithoutContext,"/NodeList/0/$ns3::TcpL4Protocol/SocketList/0
/CongestionWindow",MakeCallback(&CwndTracer));

  NS_LOG_INFO ("Configure␣Tracing.");
  AsciiTraceHelper ascii;
  PointToPointHelper ptp;
  ptp.EnableAsciiAll (ascii.CreateFileStream("tcp.tr"));

  // Simulation.
  NS_LOG_INFO ("Running␣Simulation..");
  Simulator::Stop (Seconds(1000));
  Simulator::Run ();
  Simulator::Destroy ();
  NS_LOG_INFO ("Done!.");
}
```

C.8   SIMULATING CLASSICAL QUEUEING MODELS IN NS-3

We will use this small example (thanks to M. Lacage) for showing how we can simulate a M/M/1 queue with NS-3.

The author creates two classes: a Queue and a Sender. The Receiver is only a static method which prints the packets received. When simulation starts, the Sender will send packets each "send-Interval" to the Queue that will Enqueue them and treat them a "serviceDuration" time; when it finishes, it sends the packets to the receiver method.

Listing C.3: C++ program for M/M/1 simulation in NS-3 (from M. Lacage).

```cpp
#include "ns3/packet.h"
#include "ns3/ptr.h"
#include "ns3/random-variable.h"
#include "ns3/callback.h"
#include "ns3/simulator.h"
#include "ns3/nstime.h"
#include "ns3/command-line.h"
#include <list>

using namespace ns3;
using namespace std;

class Queue
{
```

```
public:
  void SetServiceDuration (RandomVariable v);
  void SetReceiver (Callback<void,Ptr<Packet> > receiver);
  void Enqueue (Ptr<Packet> p);
private:
  void StartWork (void);
  void EndWork (Ptr<Packet> work);
  Callback<void,Ptr<Packet> > m_receiver;
  std::list<Ptr<Packet> > m_queue;
  EventId m_working;
  RandomVariable m_random;
};
void
Queue::SetServiceDuration (RandomVariable v)
{
  m_random = v;
}
void
Queue::SetReceiver (Callback<void,Ptr<Packet> > receiver)
{
  m_receiver = receiver;
}
void
Queue::Enqueue (Ptr<Packet> p)
{
  std::cout << Simulator::Now ().GetSeconds () << " " << m_queue.size ()
            << std::endl;
  m_queue.push_back (p);
  if (!m_working.IsRunning ())
    {
      StartWork ();
    }
}
void
Queue::StartWork (void)
{
  double serviceDuration = m_random.GetValue ();
  Ptr<Packet> work = m_queue.front ();
  m_queue.pop_front ();
  m_working = Simulator::Schedule (Seconds (serviceDuration),
                                   &Queue::EndWork, this, work);
}
```

```
void
Queue::EndWork (Ptr<Packet> work)
{
  m_receiver (work);
  if (!m_queue.empty ())
    {
      StartWork ();
    }
}


class Sender
{
public:
  void SetCreationInterval (RandomVariable v);
  void SetPacketSize (uint32_t v);
  void SetReceiver (Callback<void,Ptr<Packet> > receiver);
  void Start (void);
  void Stop (void);
private:
  void DoSend (void);
  RandomVariable m_creationInterval;
  uint32_t m_packetSize;
  Callback<void,Ptr<Packet> > m_receiver;
  EventId m_sending;
};
void
Sender::DoSend (void)
{
  uint32_t nbytes = m_packetSize;
  Ptr<Packet> p = Create<Packet> (nbytes);
  m_receiver (p);
  double sendInterval = m_creationInterval.GetValue ();
  m_sending = Simulator::Schedule (Seconds (sendInterval),
                                   &Sender::DoSend, this);
}
void
Sender::SetCreationInterval (RandomVariable v)
{
  m_creationInterval = v;
}
void
Sender::SetPacketSize (uint32_t v)
```

```
{
  m_packetSize = v;
}
void
Sender::SetReceiver (Callback<void,Ptr<Packet> > receiver)
{
  m_receiver = receiver;
}
void
Sender::Start (void)
{
  DoSend ();
}
void
Sender::Stop (void)
{
  m_sending.Cancel ();
}

static void Receiver (Ptr<Packet> p)
{
 std::cout << Simulator::Now ().GetSeconds () << "Get=" << p->GetSize ()
           << std::endl;
}

int main (int argc, char *argv[])
{
   unsigned int rep = 1;
   double lambda = 9.0;
   double mu = 10.0;
   double tmax = 100000.0;

  CommandLine cmd;
  cmd.AddValue ("rep", "Rep", rep);
  cmd.AddValue ("l", "Lambda", lambda);
  cmd.AddValue ("mu", "mu", mu);
  cmd.AddValue ("tmax", "Tmax", tmax );

  cmd.Parse (argc,argv);

  SeedManager::SetRun(rep);
```

```
Queue *queue = new Queue ();
queue->SetServiceDuration (ExponentialVariable (1.0/mu));
queue->SetReceiver (MakeCallback (&Receiver));
Sender *sender = new Sender ();
sender->SetCreationInterval (ExponentialVariable (1.0/lambda));
sender->SetPacketSize (1000);
sender->SetReceiver (MakeCallback (&Queue::Enqueue, queue));
Simulator::Schedule (Seconds (0.0001), &Sender::Start, sender);
Simulator::Schedule (Seconds (tmax), &Sender::Stop, sender);
Simulator::Run ();
Simulator::Destroy ();
delete sender;
delete queue;
return 0;
}
```

Bibliography

[1] *GAWK: Effective AWK Programming: A User's Guide for GNU Awk, for the 3.1.8 (or later) version of the GNU implementation of AWK.* Cited on page(s) 31

[2] Ns-3 doxigen documentation. `http://www.nsnam.org/docs/release/ns-3.11/doxygen/index.html`. Cited on page(s) 151

[3] *Ns-3 Manual.* `http://www.nsnam.org/docs/release/ns-3.11/manual/singlehtml/index.html`. Cited on page(s) 153, 155

[4] *PERL – Practical Extraction and Report Language.* Cited on page(s) 33

[5] Tclcl web page. `http://otcl-tclcl.sourceforge.net/tclcl/`. Cited on page(s) 5

[6] A. M. Viterbi, A. J. Viterbi, and E. Zehavi. Performance of power-controlled wideband terrestrial digital communication. *IEEE Transactions on Communications*, 4(41):559–569, April 1993. DOI: 10.1109/26.223780 Cited on page(s) 146

[7] M. Allman, S. Dawkins, D. Glover, J. Griner, D. Tran, T. Henderson, J. Heidemann, J. Touch, H. Kruse, S. Ostermann, K. Scott, and J. Semke. Request for comments rfc-2760: Ongoing tcp research related to satellites. 2000. Cited on page(s) 2

[8] E. Altman. A stateless approach for improving tcp performance using diffserv. In *Proceedings of the 18th International Teletraffic Congress*, September 2003. Berlin, 31 Aug - 5 Sept. Cited on page(s) 95, 100

[9] E. Altman and T. Jiménez. Novel delayed ack techniques for improving tcp performance in multihop wireless networks. In *PWC (Personal Wireless Communications)*, volume 2775/2003, pages 237–250. LNCS, Springer Berlin/Heidelberg, September 2003. Venice, Italy. DOI: 10.1007/978-3-540-39867-7_26 Cited on page(s) 126

[10] E. Altman and T. Jiménez. Simulation analysis of red with short lived tcp connection. *Computer Networks*, 44(5):631–641, April 2004. DOI: 10.1016/j.comnet.2003.08.003 Cited on page(s) 94

[11] Todd R. Andel and ALec Yasinasac. On the credibility of manet simulations. *IEEE Computer Magazine*, 2006. DOI: 10.1109/MC.2006.242 Cited on page(s) 5

[12] L. Andrew, C. Marcondes, S. Floyd, L. Dunn, R. Guillier, W. Gang, L. Eggert, S. Ha, and I. Rhee. Towards a common tcp evaluation suite. In *PFLDnet*, March 2008. Cited on page(s) 2

[13] A. Ballardie. Core Based Trees (CBT) Multicast Routing Architecture. RFC 2201 (Historic), September 1997. Cited on page(s) 69

[14] T. Bonald and J. Roberts. Performance modeling of elastic trafic in overload. In *ACM Sigmetrics*, pages 342–343, 2001. DOI: 10.1145/384268.378845 Cited on page(s) 101, 145

[15] B. Braden, D. Clark, J. Crowcroft, B. Davie, S. Deering, D. Estrin, S. Floyd, V. Jacobson, G. Minshall, C. Partridge, L. Peterson, K. Ramakrishnan, S. Shenker, J. Wroclawski, and L. Zhang. Recommendations on Queue Management and Congestion Avoidance in the Internet. RFC 2309 (Informational), April 1998. Cited on page(s) 77

[16] Josh Broch, David A. Maltz, David B. Johnson, Yih chun Hu, and Jorjeta Jetcheva. A performance comparison of multi-hop wireless ad hoc network routing protocols. pages 85–97, 1998. DOI: 10.1145/288235.288256 Cited on page(s) 2

[17] Xi Chen, Siu chung Wong, Chi K. Tse, and Francis C. M. Lau. Oscillation and period doubling in tcp/red system: Analysis and verification. *International Journal of Bifurcation and Chaos*, 18(5):1459–1475, 2008. DOI: 10.1142/S0218127408021105 Cited on page(s) 2

[18] D. D. Clark and W. Fang. Explicit allocation of best-e ort packet delivery service. *IEEE/ACM Trans on Networking*, 6(4):362–373, August 1998. DOI: 10.1109/90.720870 Cited on page(s) 96

[19] M. S. Corson, S. Papademetriou, P. Papadopolous, V. D. Park, and A. Qayyum. An internet manet encapsulation protocol (imep) specification. Internet draft, draft-ietf-manet-imep-spec01.txt, August 1998. Cited on page(s) 111

[20] M. Crovella and A. Bestravos. Self-similarity in world wide web traffic: Evidence and possible cause. *ACM Sigmetrics*, 1996. DOI: 10.1145/233008.233038 Cited on page(s) 51, 145

[21] T. V. Lakshman D. P. Heyman and A. L. Neidhardt. A new method for analysing feedback-based protocols with applications to engineering web traffic over the internet. In *ACM Sigmetrics*, 1997. DOI: 10.1145/258623.258670 Cited on page(s) 146

[22] S. Deering, D. Estrin, D. Farinacci, Ching-Gung Liu V. Jacobson, and L. Wei. An architecture for wise-area multicast routing. Technical Report USC-SC-94-565, Computer Science Department, University of Southern California, 1994. Cited on page(s) 69

[23] ETSI. Universal mobile telecommunication system (umts); selection procedures for the choice of radio transmission technologies of the umts. UMTS 30.03 Version 3.2.0, April 1998.

Available (public domain) at `http://www.etsi.org/getastandard/home.htm`. Cited on page(s) 145

[24] K. Fall and K. Varadhan. The ns manual. available at `http://www.isi.edu/nsnam/ns/`. Cited on page(s) 68

[25] Kevin Fall and Sally Floyd. Simulation-based comparisons of tahoe, reno, and sack tcp. *Computer Communication Review*, 26(3):5–21, July 1996. DOI: 10.1145/235160.235162 Cited on page(s) 1

[26] W. Fang, N. Seddigh, and B. Nandy. A Time Sliding Window Three Colour Marker (TSWTCM). RFC 2859 (Experimental), June 2000. Cited on page(s) 99

[27] M. Fleury, G. Flores Lucio, and M. J. Reed. Clarification of the ?opnet ns-2 comparison. Cited on page(s) 4

[28] Sally Floyd and Van Jacobson. Random early detection gateways for congestion avoidance. *IEEE/ACM Trans. Netw.*, 1:397–413, August 1993. DOI: 10.1109/90.251892   Cited on page(s) 77, 78

[29] Zhenghua Fu, Haiyun Luo, Petros Zerfos, Songwu Lu, Lixia Zhang, and Mario Gerla. The impact of multihop wireless channel on tcp throughput and loss. In *IEEE INFOCOM*, pages 1744–1753, 2003. DOI: 10.1109/INFCOM.2003.1209197 Cited on page(s) 126, 130

[30] P. Pablo Garrido, Manuel P. Malumbres, and Carlos T. Calafate. ns-2 vs. opnet: a comparative study of the ieee 802.11e technology on manet environments. In *Proceedins of SIMUTools*, Marseille, France, March 03–07 2008. Cited on page(s) 4

[31] Christoph Hanle and Markus Hofmann. Performance comparison of reliable multicast protocols using the network simulator ns-2. In *PROCEEDINGS OF THE ANNUAL CONFERENCE ON LOCAL COMPUTER NETWORKS*, 1998. DOI: 10.1109/LCN.1998.727663 Cited on page(s) 2

[32] J. Heinanen, F. Baker, W. Weiss, and J. Wroclawski. Assured Forwarding PHB Group. RFC 2597 (Proposed Standard), June 1999. Updated by RFC 3260. Cited on page(s) 95

[33] J. Heinanen and R. Guerin. A Two Rate Three Color Marker. RFC 2698 (Informational), September 1999. Cited on page(s) 99

[34] Thomas R. Henderson, Sumit Roy, Sally Floyd, and George D. Riley. ns-3 project goals. DOI: 10.1145/1190455.1190468 Cited on page(s) 3

[35] Christian. Huitema. *Routing in the Internet / Christian Huitema*. Prentice Hall PTR, Englewood Cliffs, N.J. :, 1995. Cited on page(s) 65

[36] Murat M iran Köksal. A survey of network simulators supporting wireless networks. In *Available on the Internet.* Cited on page(s) 3

[37] V. Jacobson. Congestion avoidance and control. *In* ACM SIGCOMM 88,, pages 273–288, 1988. DOI: 10.1145/52325.52356 Cited on page(s) 41

[38] D. Johnson, Y. Hu, and D. Maltz. The Dynamic Source Routing Protocol (DSR) for Mobile Ad Hoc Networks for IPv4. RFC 4728 (Experimental), February 2007. Cited on page(s) 111

[39] Leonard Kleinrock. *Theory, Volume 1, Queueing Systems.* Wiley-Interscience, 1975. Cited on page(s) 133

[40] Gilberto Flores Lucio, Marcos Paredes-farrera, Emmanuel Jammeh, Martin Fleury, and Martin J. Reed. Opnet modeler and ns-2: Comparing the accuracy of network simulators for packet-level analysis using a network testbed. In *3rd WEAS International Conference on Simulation, Modelling and Optimization (ICOSMO)*, pages 700–707, 2003. Cited on page(s) 4

[41] Marek Malowidzki. Network simulators: A developer?s perspective. In *International Symposium on Performance Evaluation of Computer and Telecommunication Systems (SPECTS?04)*, 2004. Cited on page(s) 3

[42] A. Mankin, A. Romanow, S. Bradner, and V. Paxon. Rfc 2357: Ietf criteria for evaluating reliable multicast transport and application protocols. 1998. Cited on page(s) 2

[43] W. Noureddine and F. Tobagi. Improving the performance of interactive tcp applications using service differentiation. In *IEEE Infocom*, 2002. DOI: 10.1109/INFCOM.2002.1019243 Cited on page(s) 100

[44] D. Park and M. S. Corson. Temporally-ordered routing algorithm (tora) version 1: functional specifications. Internet draft, July 2001. From; `http://tools.ietf.org/html/draft-ietf-manet-tora-spec-04`. Cited on page(s) 111

[45] V. D. Park and M. S. Corson. A performance comparison of the temporally-ordered routing algorithm and ideal link-state routing. In *Proceedings of the Third IEEE Symposium on Computers & Communications*, pages 592–, Washington, DC, USA, 1998. IEEE Computer Society. DOI: 10.1109/ISCC.1998.702600 Cited on page(s) 111

[46] C. Perkins, E. Belding-Royer, and S. Das. Ad hoc On-Demand Distance Vector (AODV) Routing. RFC 3561 (Experimental), July 2003. Cited on page(s) 111

[47] Charles E. Perkins and Pravin Bhagwat. Highly dynamic destination-sequenced distance-vector routing (dsdv) for mobile computers. In *Proceedings of the conference on Communications architectures, protocols and applications*, SIGCOMM '94, pages 234–244, New York, NY, USA, 1994. ACM. DOI: 10.1145/190809.190336 Cited on page(s) 111

[48] Peter Pieda, Jeremy Ethridge, Mandeep Baines, and Farhan Shallwani. *A Network Simulator, Differentiated Services Implementation.* Open IP, Nortel Networks, 2000. Cited on page(s) 95

[49] J. Postel and J. Reynolds. File transfer protocol. RFC 959 (Standard), October 1985. Updated by RFCs 2228, 2640, 2773, 3659, 5797. Cited on page(s) 17

[50] Sheldon Ross. *Simulation.* Academic Press, 4th edition, 2002. Cited on page(s) 150

[51] R. Gummadi S. Floyd and S. Shenker. Adaptive red: an algorithm for increasing the robustness of red's active queue management. from: http://www.icir.org/floyd/red.html, 2001. Cited on page(s) 79

[52] Sambit Sahu, Philippe Nain, Christophe Diot, Victor Firoiu, and Don Towsley. On achievable service differentiation with token bucket marking for TCP. In *Proceedings of the 2000 ACM SIG-METRICS international conference on Measurement and modeling of computer systems*, SIGMET-RICS '00, pages 23–33, New York, NY, USA, 2000. ACM. DOI: 10.1145/339331.339342 Cited on page(s) 102

[53] S Shah, A Khandre, M. Shirole, and G . Bhole. Performance evaluation of ad hoc routing protocols using ns2 simulation. In *Mobile and Pervasive Computing (CoMPC)*, 07=08 Aug 2008. DOI: 10.1016/j.comcom.2007.02.015 Cited on page(s) 2

[54] Biplab Sikdar, S. Kalyanaraman, and Kenneth S. Vastola. An integrated model for the latency and steady-state throughput of tcp connections. *Perform. Eval.*, 46:139–154, October 2001. DOI: 10.1016/S0166-5316(01)00048-7 Cited on page(s) 51, 52, 101, 109, 145

[55] P. Sinha. *Routing and transport layer protocols for wireless networks.* PhD thesis, Univ. of Illinois at Urbana-Champaign, Computer Science, 2001. Cited on page(s) 126

[56] D. Thaler. Border Gateway Multicast Protocol (BGMP): Protocol Specification. RFC 3913 (Historic), September 2004. Cited on page(s) 69

[57] D. Waitzman, C. Partridge, and S.E. Deering. Distance Vector Multicast Routing Protocol. RFC 1075 (Experimental), November 1988. Cited on page(s) 69

[58] Xiaodong Xian, Weiren Shi, and He Huang. Comparison of OMNET++ and other simulator for WSN simulation. DOI: 10.1109/ICIEA.2008.4582757 Cited on page(s) 4

Authors' Biographies

EITAN ALTMAN

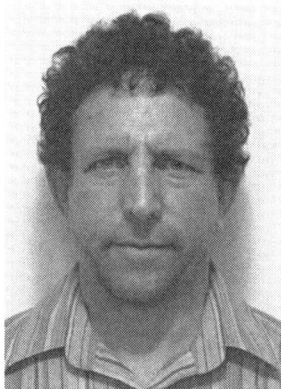

Eitan Altman received the B.Sc. in electrical engineering (1984), the B.A. degree in physics (1984) and the Ph.D. degree in electrical engineering (1990), all from the Technion-Israel Institute, Haifa. In (1990) he further received his B.Mus. degree in music composition at Tel-Aviv University. Since 1990, he has been with INRIA Sophia-Antipolis, France. His current research interests include performance evaluation and control of telecommunication networks and in particular, wireless communications and networking games. He is in the editorial board of the journals: DGAA (Dynamic Games and Applications) and JEDC, and served in the editorial board of the journals Stochastic Models, COMNET, SIAM SICON, WINET and JDEDs. He has been the general chairman and the (co)chairman of the program committee of several international conferences and workshops (on game theory, networking games and mobile networks). He is the steering committee chair of WIOPT and of NetGCoop and a Fellow member of IEEE. For more information see `www-sop.inria.fr/members/Eitan.Altman`.

TANIA JIMÉNEZ

Tania Jiménez received her Ph.D. from University of Nice Sophia-Antipolis, France in 2000. She was Assistant Professor at Universidad de Los Andes, Venezuela from 2000 to 2002, in the Center of Models and Simulation (CeSiMo). She is at present a research engineer at Avignon University, in the Informatics Lab (`http://lia.univ-avignon.fr`). Her research interests include simulation as well as optimization and control of telecommunication networks.

CPSIA information can be obtained at www.ICGtesting.com
Printed in the USA
BVOW080548080312

284704BV00004B/1/P

9 781608 456925